TRUE NORTH

Diary of a North Country Year

TRUE NORTH

Diary of a North Country Year

STEPHEN J. KRASEMANN

NorthWord
PRESS, INC
Box 1360, Minocqua, WI 54548

*This book
is dedicated
to wild places
and all
critters that
live there.*

N

A fallen birch tree is
complemented by colorful
autumn reflections in the water.

© 1992 Stephen J. Krasemann
Published by:
NorthWord Press, Inc.
P.O. Box 1360
Minocqua, WI 54548

ISBN 1-55971-176-0

Edited by Greg Linder
Consulting Editor: Susan K. Cook
Designed by Russell S. Kuepper

For a free catalog describing NorthWord's line of books
and gift items, call toll free 1-800-336-5666.

Printed in Singapore.

Library of Congress Cataloging-in-Publication Data

Krasemann, Stephen J.
        True north : diary of a North Country year / Stephen J. Krasemann.
            p.   cm.
        ISBN 1-55971-176-0
        1. Nature photography.   I. Title.
    TR721.K723   1992
    770'.92--dc20
    [B]   92-17192
                                                                  CIP

A NORTH COUNTRY YEAR

Introduction 8

APRIL
Will Spring Never Come? 10

MAY
Tracks in the Sand 20

JUNE
The Moose Attack 34

JULY
Good-bye, All You Loons 50

AUGUST
The Gift of the Fox 60

SEPTEMBER
The Grizzly Encounter 72

OCTOBER
Spirits in the Forest 84

NOVEMBER
Between Light and Darkness 96

DECEMBER
The Hibernators Have It Right 108

JANUARY
More to Snow Than Meets the Eye .. 118

FEBRUARY
The Chickadee Forecasts 130

MARCH
The Standoff 138

APRIL
Final Visions 152

INTRODUCTION

I begin this book in the first season of my year, in spring, as life is beginning anew in the northern forest. Sometime in April, when light returns and the sun radiates warmth, there commences a time of promise for the year ahead, a time of welcoming all the ambience of new life into myself.

I lived in and traveled through the north-woods for this book.

I watched the full leaves of summer turn into gold and fly off in gentle breezes.

I watched the snows drift high, then settle into puddles on the soft earth.

I witnessed misting ice storms, soft falling clumps of snowflake bundles, driving rains, and the foggy breaths of dewy condensation.

I experienced extremes, from searing heat and stifling humidity to bitter cold with oppressive wind; from endless days to black nights illuminated by countless stars.

I traveled from Maine all through Canada and across the United States to the Great Lakes, then again into the northern and western mountains of North America.

Back and forth, in every season, I drove to random destinations of my choice in my pickup truck and camper. Many of these were jumping-off points for other means of travel—by canoe, by foot, by horseback.

At the onset of the project, I scribbled a list of what makes the northwoods special to me—what sets it apart from other environments. I called the list "Northwoods Ingredients," and I listed these ingredients to sum up the sort of subjects or feelings I must photograph and write about in order to present a relatively complete package.

The list, in no particular order, includes: orchids, waterfalls, white pines, moose and whitetail deer, black flies and mosquitoes, changing seasons, spring wildflowers, autumn maples, icy lakeshores, birches and tamaracks, the smells of the forest, red squirrels, red foxes, mountains, places where one can escape from human signs and sounds, blue jays and gray jays, mosses and exposed rocks, loons (of course), bald eagles, snowshoe hares, warblers, Canada geese, hummingbirds, martens, lynx, elk, and wolves. And lots of water—black-water streams, green-fringed bogs, and bright blue lakes.

When I wasn't traveling, I returned to my cabin near the north shore of Lake Superior, in the heart of "the land of the raven." During my stays I edited slides and writings while soaking in life around the cabin. I went for many walks, for many reasons—to be in the wind, to look for animals and flowers, to simply get back in touch with my thoughts, to take a time-out away from a faster pace. I enjoyed looking, finding little things, discovering moments that pleased my eye and my heart.

This book is a celebration, distilling what I observed and felt and heard and discovered . . . special moments for you, the reader.

With this, let me begin.

APRIL Will Spring Never Come?

April 7

I am at the cabin window, looking out over the landscape. Snow is melting with the soothing, cool warmth of spring. The thermometer rises above freezing every day, but still I find little new plant growth, even when I scrape away the dead leaves on the forest floor. Other signs tell me my wait for new growth will end soon—aspen catkins are fattening, and red osier dogwood limbs protrude from the snowbanks, as bright as sticks of red licorice.

How many minds have wondered if spring will never come?

April 9

Flies are buzzing on warmed, sheltered walls, and the first ants of the season poke tentatively about. The flies buzz and settle in patches of sunlight.

It was 75 degrees yesterday; it's 45 degrees today. Severe weather is spawned when hot and cold air masses collide. Indeed, there is a severe weather watch until 8 p.m. tonight, with a chance of hail, damaging winds, and lightning. It's pouring rain at the moment.

A male evening grosbeak perches amidst new spring tamarack needles.

April 12

New buds are barely bursting on weeping willows and some maples, although the leaves are coated with wet, stick-to-the-branches snow. Last night, northerly winds plastered thick globs of flakes against the north sides of trees, while temperatures dipped to just below freezing.

As spring would have it, clearing skies this morning slant

New snow covers fallen branches in Wisconsin's Kettle Moraine State Park.

warm sun onto the alabaster landscape. Almost immediately, the temperature is in the 40s. Photographically, I race against the sun's warmth, which is softening the snow, and the southerly breezes that rattle it off the branches.

Two hours later, seeing the wet vegetation, one wouldn't even know there was snow rather than rain last night.

April 15

The snow plays hide-and-seek with the brilliant sun. Patches of frost lie in small pockets of grass where warming rays have not yet reached. While much of the soil bubbles and gurgles as it thaws, sending up the pungent aroma of earth, the ground remains frozen solid on the north side of knolls and hillocks.

It's only a matter of time before the sun discovers these patches, too.

April 22

The dawn light brightens the pond outside the cabin while I sit quietly, sipping hot chamomile tea with honey. A singing robin briefly—but quite energetically—intrudes on the silence. Then it's quiet again.

A pair of Canada geese swim along the shore, rippling the waters to shimmer in shades of gray, blue, and orange as the sunrise approaches. Two more geese skim the pond's surface, splashing down noisily with a chorus of honks as they join the other geese.

Now a chickadee sings; in the distance, a grouse drums. I can feel a breeze pushing. The surface

Canada goose parents escort three goslings on a swim over white-pine water reflections.

LEFT: Vestiges of this snowshoe hare's white winter fur are still visible.

OVERLEAF: A mountain goat grazes in paradise, known to humans as Glacier National Park.

of the lake no longer reflects the shoreline trees. The light is bright enough so that I can see green from the grasses, red from the osiers, and yellow from the new willow leaves.

My tea is finished. My drifting thoughts have returned, and breakfast is beckoning me.

April 25

It has been raining for days. I laid down this afternoon to take a nap; then the sun came out!

Two bobcat kittens peer beyond the edge of their world.

It was late afternoon, and the rays slanted over the moss and the trees, lending wonderful texture and contrast to the beautiful, rich greens. Without a moment's thought, I decided I'd better take my photographs while the sun lasted. So I jumped up.

But it was not sunny. It had all been a dream. First all the rain, then a dream about the sun—too much.

April 27

Shortly after sunset, I walk outdoors to fetch an armful of wood. As I step out the door, I freeze. A snowshoe hare, still white-legged, sits alert.

Slowly easing away, the hare approaches my woodpile. As it nears the pile it suddenly bolts at the wood, kicks the side of the pile with its hind feet, and glances off into the air, landing five feet distant.

I've seen this behavior before. The hare was testing the pile for a hidden predator that might have been crouching behind the logs, waiting for the snowshoe to come within range.

The hare's ploy was to startle the predator into action (the hare would already be running away) or into recoiling (the hare would then hear or see the predator, and would also keep going).

This time there is no predator; the hare returns and begins eating grasses growing near the woodpile. Its feeding is undisturbed, even though I watch.

OVERLEAF: Many Glacier Landscape, Glacier National Park, broods in the high winds so common on the eastern Rocky Mountain front range.

RIGHT: Avalanche lilies thrive on or near the snowline.

MAY Tracks in the Sand

May 3

I'm sitting on the open porch. My eyes trace the dendritic branches of still-leafless trees into the clear night sky, and farther on to the stars of the Milky Way. I'm perched outside simply to get back in touch with my thoughts.

My father lives in the northwoods of Wisconsin. When I was a teenager living at home, I often walked outside at night to peer into the sky, pondering the significant thoughts of a teenager entering the adult world.

When a crucial decision about life's direction was distilling in my mind, I would gaze into the night, hoping for a definitive light to illuminate the answer in my mind.

On those crystal-clear nights, with so many wondrous stars, I seemed able to work with my facts and feelings. Somehow an answer often appeared as I watched.

Some 20 years later I still wander outdoors when I visit my dad, looking into the sky, remembering nights of years ago, and knowing some of my decisions turned out successfully.

The aptly named, twisting waters of Snake Pit Falls in Wisconsin.

May 4

Tonight I walked at dusk. Spring has gingerly arrived, but there are no pesky bugs out . . . yet.

I hiked to the beaver pond and watched a beaver swim closer and closer until it realized that my shape was foreign amidst the familiar landmarks.

KARSLAPP! Its alarm sounded across the water like a rifle shot, and the beaver dived

Freed from the confines of ice, a beaver nibbles on a sprig of willow.

Sunlight beams through the trees in a red pine forest.

beneath the splash it created, reappearing only to repeat its act several more times before calming.

I strolled into young groves of spruce and pine. Scanning little trees, I tried to judge which junior trees would survive the upward competition for light. I nosed up to a spruce flower, to see how much pollen had gathered on the new cone lips. And I watched for my favorite plants—a tamarack or birch beginning to grow, or a white pine or daisy patch taking hold.

May 7

In vegetation, the onset of photosynthesis takes place at about 43 degrees Fahrenheit. The early spring in the woods fosters "short-day" wild-flowers—violets, bloodroots, marsh marigolds, and anemones. These flowers have short stems, require little time to grow stamens and pistils, and become ready to pollinate and form seeds in the short time before the growing leaves of the forest cut off life-giving sun.

Later the "long-day" flowers appear. Columbines, roses, and irises appear along forest openings and at the edges of fields, and need additional time to lengthen their stems. Their bloom schedule centers on June 21st, the longest day of the year.

May 10

A year ago today, 22 inches of snow fell on Michigan's Upper Peninsula. Today, as I drove to the U.P., the temperature was 83 degrees—hot to my body after recent 50-degree days.

Along the south shore of Lake Superior, spring is at the point of bursting into summer. The woods are carpeted with spring beauty, and trout lilies are opening like yellow popcorn. The plant growth is rapidly drawing moisture from the soil. At the top of knolls, the soil is dry enough to sit on without receiving a wet butt, but that's not true halfway down the waterless drainage. Young maple trees of varying heights (in inches, not feet) sprout abundantly among all the wildflowers. When I kick dry leaves, I hear the sound of autumn.

May 11

I did a scratch-and-sniff with a balsam needle. It smelled a lovely pine-sap odor. While I knelt with dirt-stained knees, photographing Dutchman's breeches, several black flies landed on my neck, looking for an early meal.

May 12

A slight frosting of yellow-green is hazing the distant hills, although no leaves are out on the trees—only bursting buds.

Chorus frogs sing at full decibel along the beaver pond fringes. Locating the source of a single voice among hundreds—if not thousands—is nearly impossible. A loud noise will cause the clamor to cease. But after a few moments of silence the first hearty trill is sounded, and soon the entire chorus is singing once again.

A person could quite literally go mad or lose his hearing with prolonged immersion in the din of these inch-long frogs. Their call has the ping of discordant steel being hammered—not unlike the uncomfortable edge of fingers scratched on a blackboard. But at a distance, I love the flavor these little songsters add to the spring night.

May 16

Driving back to the cabin I wondered, "When does spring end?"

Surely we all agree that the longest seasons are winter and summer, and that spring and autumn are much too short. But if so, why are we so eager for spring and fall to pass into summer

A "skipper" butterfly feeds on a daisy.

and winter?

Spring has been happening here in various forms for almost a month, with no end in sight. Buds are still unfurling. Hummingbirds and swallows have yet to arrive. And most birds must still build their nests.

I would guess that there is at least a month of spring remaining. Shouldn't we cherish this season a mite longer before our headlong rush into summer?

May 17

High temperatures in the 50s. Today I saw my first male ruby-throated hummingbird, my first male and female rose-breasted grosbeaks, and the first baby red squirrel of the season.

This is the second day in a row that it rained all day. All the ponds are full, and little puddles have formed throughout the woods—the better

RIGHT: An immature ruby-throated hummingbird perches above a ripe raspberry.

to hatch mosquitoes.

A few additional blooms have opened in the marsh marigold patch. Ever so slightly, green is spreading across the distant hillside. With a few 75-degree days, the countryside will burst into leaf.

May 18

This book gives me another excuse to discover and explore new areas. Tonight I'm walking to a waterfall on the Pine River in Ontario. After recent rains, the falls are boiling into mists.

As the sun sets and the falls settle into shade, the opposite bank remains sunlit, creating a few moments of sensuous light on the miniature side-water flows. There's just barely enough time for me to expose 15 frames of Kodachrome.

May 19

Two male evening grosbeaks veer into my cabin window, stunning themselves as they bounce off onto a bed of spent needles under a large spruce tree.

I run outside, picking one up, and it immediately flies into the forest. But the other grosbeak could be a domestic pet, the way he perches on my finger as I carry him to a protected corner. Several minutes later, his body tenses. His eyes become alert to birds flying by, and his interest focuses on the cry of a distant kestrel.

A red squirrel pauses in a rare moment of rest.

LEFT: The waterfall at Wilmington Notch, Adirondack Mountains.

After one more brief moment, he launches into the spruce, pauses for several minutes, then disappears through the air.

May 20

As I depart for a walk this afternoon, I see a painted turtle on the grass, conspicuously out of place. I notice freshly dug earth, and I figure that the turtle might be laying eggs.

Sure enough. She's dug a hole many inches deep. I can't tell how far it goes, because a layer of speckled eggs fills the cup-shaped hole to within four inches of the top.

While I watch, she pulls her head into her shell and lets a pure white egg fall into the hole. It's then I realize that the speckled eggs in the hole are speckled with flecks of dirt, from tumbling into their earthen chamber.

All told, I watch seven additional eggs fill the nest before the turtle stretches her hind legs, reaching out to pull freshly dug, sandy earth over the eggs. For thirty minutes, she packs the earth and scratches the ground level, so nothing will give the site away to a skunk or some other predator.

I wonder. Once these eggs hatch, how will the little turtles find their way to the small river 100 yards distant? Spending their new life energy, how long will it take them to get through the tall grasses, even if they unerringly travel in the correct direction?

May 21

I depart Ontario, heading south along the north shore of Lake Superior. I'm beginning to sort through the items that shake loose in the camper, and in a few days I'll have a working system. All items that I don't use daily will be pushed deeper into the less accessible areas under the bed, or stashed at the bottom of boxes.

For now it's a continuing search. Move this. Where did I put that? Pull out, put away.

I'm ten hours down the road, and I've stopped along the way to photograph pussywillows heavy with pollen in a stand of young birch.

Moose seek ponds in summer for fresh aquatic vegetation and for solace from biting insects.

Tired, I stop at Gooseberry Falls, Minnesota, for the night. Spring runoff from the forest tumbles rushing water over and down, into Lake Superior. Spray rises from the falls, cooling the air and carrying with it the scent of watery freshness.

A warm feeling settles over me as I pull into the campsite this evening, having to do with the road and its adventure. I know it well. How many beautiful sunsets will I see? How many intimate wildlife encounters will I have? Who will I meet? Just the good memories, please.

I'm opening myself to the experiences of the natural world; to dwell in its active presence is to nourish my sense of being alive.

May 23

Moose antlers are beginning to sprout. Petulant squirrels sit in the spruces, verbally abusing each other. There's really nothing much the matter—little squirrels just like to chatter.

Green has arrived. So much green. Not for many months have my eyes and cameras feasted on such hues. Small, new, crinkly leaves of yellow-green; lush mosses and spruce needles regaining their vibrancy. Even the emerging needles of the tamaracks mimic small paintbrushes dipped in bright green. It seems odd that we so often use just one word—green—to describe many colors.

With warmth on the skin, bird music, and returning flowers, it's a relief to realize that a new season is here to stay.

May 24

Taking photographs is the process of either subtracting compositional elements to make the most effective image, or adding compositional elements to create the most complex image without cluttering the picture. The quantity of natural photos taken is directly related to the amount of time spent in the field.

Today is a case in point. The day begins with a lifting fog. I take a variety of photographs before the fog departs and leaves me with poor-quality, late-morning light. I'm in a new area, so I don't know where to search for photographs.

The subjects of abundance are forget-me-nots and trilliums. I discover several gatherings, but they are lit by harsh mid-day light. I venture on, and by mid-afternoon I find a hillside of trilliums, just as a cloud bank moves in. I shoot madly in the subdued light, until a clearing sky ends my fun. I keep looking for photos as the sun sinks lower; I hike, I drive, I search for images.

This is a full 14-hour day, in which my writing necessarily suffers because my photography does not. I make photographic notes, tend to exposed film, take care of cameras, load new film into my photo vest, and clean up the mess of a day's shooting. The camper tends to end up littered with jackets, vests, gloves, and film packages that went on and off as the day progressed and, finally, expired.

May 26

I'm on the sand dunes along Lake Superior in the early morning breezes, alone except for some distant ravens that were obviously here earlier—fresh tracks cover the moist sand.

When I'm photographing, I must often rise before dawn to arrive at a site during the best light. By nature, I'm a night person; I love working on projects deep into the quiet and calm of night. I resist rising in the darkness to begin my day, but I must confess that on a morning like today, I don't mind at all.

I have seen the lake do battle with the land, its waves roaring like cannons. But today, the lake barely murmurs as its waters lap the shoreline. My tracks merge with those of the ravens. In time, waves will steal them all.

LEFT: Mossy pine bogs like this one in Wisconsin make wonderful havens from summer's heat.

May 27

Perhaps its the night noises that have me lying awake at 3 a.m. Perhaps it's the hot night, or all the sun I soaked in yesterday. No matter the reason—the cool night breeze through the open window feels soothing. There's a full moon setting in the western sky; it glows yellow in the humid haze.

A Canada goose honks across the lake somewhere. Bullfrogs sound their deep baritones, a great-horned owl hoots in the distance, and a white-throated sparrow sounds just two notes of liquid song against the moonlight.

May 29

Rondeau Provincial Park in Ontario is a very dense forest of maple, ash, and beech. There are many water holes and small ponds here; it's an ideal environment for mosquitoes, and a few ply the air.

I slip into my hip boots and wade into a black-water pond to photograph water reflections, trees, and yellow buttercups. I probe for footing on submerged branches and logs, and I continually watch for reflections ahead in water I have not yet disturbed. I get a frame here, wide angle pictures to my right, then change to a macro lens to move in tighter, and use a long exposure (four seconds), ensuring depth of focus in the final photograph.

I'm moving slowly, listening to the background bird songs in the forest and concentrating on the composition of images. When I check my watch, I discover that I've lost myself in this tiny pond for over two hours.

A great horned owl stares through needled branches.

May 31

Sometimes I return to a new location two days in a row, as I'm doing today. I'm getting to know the place, discovering things I didn't notice the first day, finding new bird and animal tracks.

I'm hiking through a forest-fire burn that's three years old. I see there will be thousands of fireweed flowers here in the future, and thousands of new blueberries as well if rain continues to nurture the growing shrubs. A young forest will again stand upon this soil, all scars from the fire having healed and faded away.

This particular burn covers approximately 80 acres. A wet, creek-like drainage cuts diagonally through the land, ending in a reservoir of deep black water, ringed with deer and moose tracks. Deer are nearby, feeding on new grasses.

I can look over the waters to mountains on the horizon, then down onto the water's surface and see the same mountains reflected. I wonder how this pond might reflect the summer clouds, sunrises and sunsets, storms building, rains falling, and perhaps a rainbow.

Maybe the deer will notice.

Fireweed helps recolonize areas burned in forest fires.

JUNE The Moose Attack

June 1

The countryside is taking on a greenish haze. Before I can meet a handful of actors, the entire cast is appearing—columbine, purple violet and more, still more, each day. I see baby beavers, baby grasshoppers, warblers nesting, young gray jays, young ground squirrels, and a few mosquitoes. Strawberries bloom, and saskatoons, too. Black flies buzz, and grouse are drumming.

By the time I realize spring is actually happening, the first flowers are already losing their petals. The green haze is a curtain coming down on spring. Summer is beginning.

N

June 2

Just inside the shadows, an object flits through the air. Moments later, it pirouettes and returns. A brown bat is snatching crane flies out of the night as they buzz around my outside lamp.

Notice how long the young moose's nose will grow by adulthood.

June 3

Rain does so much for the landscape. Plants seem to grow visibly. Birds are happy, bathing in fresh puddles and filling the air with song. The early greens are suffering from the assault of mice, rabbits, and squirrels.

The past two days have seen gale winds from the south—the warmth is bringing black flies out in force, although they can't maintain their equilibrium in the wind. It's back in the

The common—but uncommonly beautiful—yellow warbler.

calm woods that the black flies wait, ever hungry. One thousand feet inside of the forest border, the wind velocity in summer is just one-tenth what it is in an open field.

There are 1,270 known species of black fly, but not all bite. If they do, it's only the female—she needs a meal of blood to nourish her developing eggs. A black fly that is about to bite attaches a series of hooks along its proboscis to the skin of its victim, making the skin nice and taut. Two razor-sharp mandibles descend from the center of the proboscis, and these begin to slash, scissors-like, digging until they hit a capillary. Blood flows into the wound; the beast vacuums up its meal, then zips away to create a few hundred more of its kind.

One black fly is generally accompanied by hundreds or thousands of fellow travelers, each frantic to fulfill its genetic destiny. They hover, dive, and loop around your head. You can lash out, but the swarm is like an apparition—your flailing arms pass right through.

June 5

It's going to be a good year for pine seed production. Spruces, pines, and tamaracks are loaded with cone flowers. Positioned upright at first to catch pollen, female cone flowers then tip upside down on their branches as they enlarge and harden into mature cones. I'm photographing a yellow warbler's nest at sunrise on this warm, breezy day. The adults show little fear of my photo blind, and both return almost immediately after the first disturbance. Once they find the nest intact, the female incubates eggs while the male patrols nearby branches for a few minutes, then flies off in search of food.

I sit with the female just long enough to take a few pictures, long enough so that she has rewarmed her eggs to temperature before I depart. I leave the area as slightly disturbed as possible.

June 6

There's something absolutely wonderful about this ability to travel across the north, up the mountains, and down into the bogs. I'm able to see localized flowers such as the ragged robin

Bunchberry, or Dwarf Cornel, in Adirondack State Park.

and painted trillium. As I travel, I also see certain plants that are typical of the northland: jack-in-the-pulpit, ram's-head lady's-slipper, and bunchberry.

My first love, though, is the far north. A rosy sunset is slipping into an Alaskan lake, and an afterglow burns behind the white pines that silhouette the horizon. All the while, no-see-um insects and black flies crawl across my skin, occasionally biting.

At this time of year, campgrounds are relatively empty; great doses of peace and privacy prevail. Later in the summer, as days warm and children are free to travel with the family, I'll go deeper into the forest for my peace. It doesn't take much walking to leave most of the crowd behind in the "civilized bush"—a mile or two usually suffices.

June 7

Today I photographed the most brilliant rainbow I've ever seen. For the first time I could see both ends, but I saw no proverbial pot of gold. Later, when I related my story, a friend suggested, "Maybe you had to dig under the rainbow's end to get to the gold." But it's too late now.

Nature offers so many beautiful moments of light, color, and shape. In my photographs, I seach for the best combinations of these elements in order to celebrate the beauty.

June 8

Standing atop a hill, I see a moose in the flats below. I set off on a photographic hike in that direction. Silently, I move to within hearing distance. A cow moose is just over the river bank, and she hasn't seen or heard me. I fire several photos before she locates the clicking of the camera. At this point I expect her to bolt, but she stands her ground. I continue photographing while she glares at me. Then she lays her ears back and raises the hair on her shoulders. It's an aggressive signal, and I proceed (quickly) to back up across the muskeg.

But I'm too late. A wobbly calf I hadn't seen bleats toward its mother, and this appears to trigger the cow into action.

A baby woodchuck—one of an annual litter
from beneath my woodshed—munches on greenery.

OVERLEAF: A rainbow arches over Denali National Park, Alaska.

She charges up and over the bank. My tripod is shiny aluminum, and she hits it head on, throwing the tripod off to the side and knocking me to the ground with her shoulder as she passes. She turns, her forefeet flailing the air, only to see the tripod laying on the ground.

Deciding that the tripod looks dead, or at least mortally wounded, she retrieves her calf and heads for parts unknown.

Meanwhile, I have rolled into some willow, freezing there, hoping she won't hear me. After a suitable interval of silence I retrieve my tripod, to find one of the legs bent and the camera lens broken. I am shaken, but unhurt. And lucky at that.

June 9

It's very windy this morning. Gusty blasts rock my tent back and forth.

I decide to climb a nearby mountain to try for pictures of bighorn ewe and lambs, but the wind is too much, quite literally. Gale forces slam me against the side of the mountain, throwing me off balance. My film, gloves, and lens caps are sent soaring. Even my tripod will be knocked over if I loosen my grip. There's no way I can photograph.

I start hiking down the other side of the mountain, and for some reason the sheep follow. I find a windbreak and take all the photographs I want.

Living a life along precipices and gaping crevices, the bighorn sheep have a remarkable sense of sure-footedness. Later, as I tediously make my safe descent across the rocky terrain, I look up to see lambs scampering across the mountain as nimbly as squirrels climbing a tree. They seem to have springs in their legs as they bounce back and forth over a resting mother. I'm aware of my own slowness, my own heaviness. They're on the moon; I'm on Jupiter.

June 13

Over the hills and through the grasses, the wind approaches, and I hear it coming. A distant murmur builds to an audible sigh, until the breeze tosses my hair and rustles all the vegetation. Lone trees suddenly dance, their branches rocking.

Wind is very much in control of comfort here. A wind off the lake is a cool wind—it sends the insects into hiding. A wind coming over the land heats the air and allows temperatures to build. It's my favorite.

The temperature is warmest in the absence of wind, but it's the worst situation because bugs are all about.

June 15

The shortest way isn't always the easiest, and topographical maps can be misleading.

I endure a painful, wicked day of walking miles over wet tussocks interspersed with marshy lowland. Progress is slow, wet, and agonizing to my feet, ankles, legs, and body.

Tussock walking is a nightmare. For every step up to the top of a tussock—a spongy mass of organic matter too wobbly to stand on but too firm to ignore—there is another step down into the narrow, clutching crevasse surrounding it. Walking across the tops, I eventually stumble and plunge into the water or, worse yet, twist my ankle. I can't sit down and I can't take off my pack, let alone prepare a meal—it's too wet, too uncomfortable, and too lumpy.

Remember the stereotypical cowboy scene in which one horseman takes another cowboy's horse and boots, then rides off and leaves the other cowboy to walk out of the desert? If so, you have a picture of how insidious tussock walking can be—except it doesn't help me if you leave my boots.

RIGHT: Mount Rundle is the most photographed of all the Canadian Rocky Mountain peaks.

All through the day I think of turning back. The last two miles are hell; I feel like crying and giving up. Finally, atop a dry ridge, I look back on that vast hummockland and pray that I'll never have to walk anything like it again.

June 18

I see the storm approaching, a gray sky overtaking me from the west until all that remains is a bright-edged slice of sky at the horizon. Rattling thunder rumbles as lightning glows in clouds, while the wind tilts the leaves to expose their undersides. I tense, for some reason, as huge dollop drops begin hitting the windows.

Without warning, a magnum-caliber blast of lightning splinters a large tree within a hundred yards. I've heard it said: "As an event draws closer, the event emits vibrations that a perceptive person can sense." Perhaps I could feel the lightning charge building. It came very close.

Now the roof sounds with hundreds, thousands, of raindrops. Thunder and sheet lightning surround the cabin, rattling windows and then rumbling off like a train steaming through a tunnel. Stray lightning bolts turn dim landscapes into bright white.

The rain slows, and the rumbling sound of thunder is replaced by the sound of blowing leaves.

June 19

This is the first heat wave of the season. Temperatures have been in the 90s for three days. Showy lady's-slippers are opening quickly in these conditions. In an hour's photography, I watch a closed, pale bud spread, exposing the pink mouth of the flower within, like a trap door opening.

Showy lady's-slipper plants are known to live more than 50 years. Since the blossom doesn't contain nectar, it's not attractive to insects, and must be cross-pollinated. Although only a small number of the flowers are pollinated each year, each will produce 15,000 to 35,000 seeds. It will take another five to six years for the seeds to produce a rhizome root system and grow into a vegetative plant—and it'll be still longer before the flowers are produced.

Whitetail deer are being pestered today by the first deerflies of the season. In weather like this, deer remain in the shady forest all day, panting as they tolerate the heat.

With the longest day of the year just two days away, the sun hangs in the sky for a long while before it lowers shade over the forest. Then, like new flowers, red-brown deer appear in the fields—a pair here, a buck with new antler prongs in the distance, another and then another, until there are ten deer grazing in this meadow.

A raven soars in turbulent skies.

LEFT: Bighorn sheep appear to be so comfortable in their rugged environment.

June 21

Today is the first day of summer and the longest of the year. And it's the day the mosquitoes emerge. Most are weak, flying erratically and bumping into their victims by accident. Mosquitoes are so fragile, but then again . . . *slap*.

June 22

All at once the cabin goes dark. I wonder what happened to the power. Then comes the thunder and crackling.

I rush outside to see a glorious, black-gray cloud mass begin to overtake the mountain. For a time, blue skies illuminate the east flank of the mountain while the black clouds close in from the west.

A minute later, trees are bent in a powerful wind. Rain pours down until the air itself seems liquid. Driving rains pound the cabin roof, and the temperature drops 20 degrees in less than five minutes.

The storm departs as quickly as it arrived, leaving daisies and dandelions disheveled. A squirrel chatters in dismay as dripping raindrops plop onto its fur.

June 23

Rain is wonderful for the plants, necessary for the summer greens of forest and meadow, and needed for replenishing water levels in lakes and ponds. But it's not so great for loons nesting at the water's edge.

Today I arrived in canoe country with an old friend, trying to relocate a loon's nest with a single egg. When I found it, it was under ten inches of water—abandoned. The lakes and bogs can't drain quickly enough.

Loons can hardly walk on land. Being water birds, their nests are basically a platform of grass at water level, allowing them to slop easily to and from the water like seals.

I was disappointed. For the past week, I'd been planning to photograph a nesting loon. I had previously located six nests, and I'd been confident that at least one would offer favorable light, composition, and cooperation from a loon. I packed, I bought supplies for eight days of wilderness photography, and I drove and then paddled many hours into lake country, only to make this rude discovery: All six nests were submerged.

Think of the loons! Some will nest, but it's too late. Even if their young hatch, they won't be big enough or strong enough to leave the lakes before freeze-up.

These things happen.

June 24

The sky is pale morning blue, and the sun warms my back as I sit atop a rock outcropping. There's a nuthatch beeping on a nearby pine, a loon calls across the lake, and a red squirrel sniffs in the mosses and lichens.

I'm enjoying the breezes in the pines; they keep the mosquitoes and black flies away. I watch the play of sunlight on the forest floor, and the slack tightropes of spider webbing as they catch pieces of sun and twist in the wind.

A chestnut-sided warbler joins the forest song of lapping waves against this island shore. Other loons call, and the nuthatch is still beeping. Suddenly I remember that I've come here for more than loon photography.

June 25

Dawn is sunny and the lake is flat, ideal conditions for canoeing. Two adult loons and a gray-black chick are on the water with me.

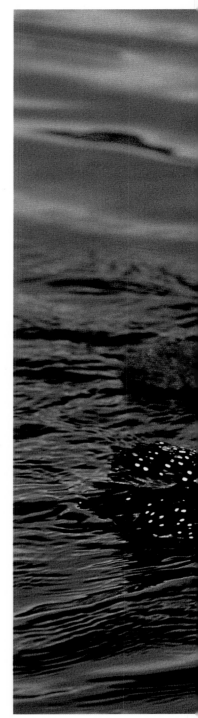

TRUE NORTH

My canoe glides nearer; my paddle strokes are smooth and slow. The adults do not flatten against the water as most loons do to avoid being seen. Nor is there an aggressive, dance-threat display on the water as a diversionary ploy. Instead, the young peaceably paddles toward me with parents in tow.

The adults begin to fish. First one dives while the other parent watches the chick and my canoe. Soon both parents dive—short trips at first, then longer ones until all parties become comfortable with our distance from one another. The adults seem to be catching small crustaceans and nymphs, or larvae of water insects.

The loon's fledging success is often relatively low due to fluctuating water levels, boating disturbance, or early freeze-ups.

With a cooing sound, all foodstuffs are immediately offered to the accepting young. An occasional crayfish or large minnow, too bulky for the chick, is swallowed by the parent with a toss of the head.

Later, after eight hours under the cloudless sky, I'm red, parched, and weary during the 2-1/2-hour paddle and portage back to camp. But exhaustion is secondary to the elation I feel at finally taking good photographs of loons.

June 26

I love paddling on still waters—the glide of a bent shaft paddle, the movement through dark water, and the rhythm of stroking while watching clouds, reflections, and birds flying overhead.

It's sunset, the time that is neither day or night. Loons call, a mysterious moon rises in the hour-long twilight, and mayflies hatch. As I take in the blues, oranges, and blacks, I know this is precisely where I should be at this given moment.

June 27

I depart at 2 p.m., after the heat of day has passed, to look for loons. As I paddle out over the first lake, I notice cirrus horsetail clouds and an obvious weather front building to the east. One must always watch the weather in canoe country.

Almost three hours and a couple of portages later, I find and photograph loons, ever watchful of the now-unstable air that raises thunderheads a good 30,000 feet. Clouds begin to thicken on the south horizon—my direction home.

Photographic light is failing and, with clouds building all around, I begin my 1-1/2-hour paddle back. Lightning starts flashing. The weather is definitely getting closer, but so is my camp.

Halfway back, I can see a squall line of rain over the hills, but that weather is moving away from me.

I slip into camp as a giant cumulo-nimbus thunderhead expands over the lake. Minutes later the cloud is split by wind shear, forming into the shape of a lumbering serpent hovering over the lake. Cold wind precedes a black sheet of distant rain so thick that it obscures each successive hill as it blows closer.

Whitecaps form in moments. Pines bend into each other, pieces of torn branches falling to the ground, while rain drills my tent. Lightning cracks, and there's instant, intense thunder. Just as quickly, the wind calms, the lightning grows distant, and a slow, steady rain settles in.

An hour later, stars fill the sky. The air is so damp and cool that I can see my breath, and a band of brightness lingers in the western sky.

June 28

A storm with lightning, thunder, and 1-1/2 inches of rainfall passed through in the early a.m. All day, clearing winds pushed whitecaps into foam against our island. By nightfall, the winds were slowing.

At 11 p.m. the sun has set, but the western sky holds color and brightness above the water and trees to our left as the bowman and I slip our canoe onto a calm lake. In the eastern sky to our right, a huge, full moon shimmers like a torch.

Slowly, quietly, we paddle, taking in the colors of sunset playing on waters from one direction and the patterns of the moon from the other direction. A loon begins to call, and it's answered by another loon somewhere toward the horizon. Back and forth, minutes are passing.

We stop paddling, and water drips like prisms from the paddle blades. I've never seen such glowing, existential light before.

This is one of those moments in which all that is beautiful about a place and an experience is realized. All the past days' suns, winds, and rains, all the loon voicing, all the paddling over rough waves and clear waters—they all come

RIGHT: A glowing sunset from my tented camp in Quetico Provincial Park, Ontario.

together. Tonight, during this short trip, the conditions combine to create a mood, a memory of canoe country. Even if we lose the details to time, we'll remember the essence.

We slip into the shadows of our island home. Moonlight disappears, and the sound of loons on the open water gives way to the lapping of waves against rocks.

If we had died moments before, we would have been in heaven.

Muted lichens encrusted on white pine bark.

June 29

If I could invent my world, it would be like today. There are raindrops on the birch leaves from last night's showers, vapors of moisture seep from the distant hills of pine across the lake, and loons are wailing, their calls echoing in stereo off the cliffs.

My views are of small mosses and lichen-covered rocks. As I watch, a squirrel climbs a pine bole, moving my view to branches against a clearing sky. Clouds mirror themselves in the lee waters in front of a nearby rocky point.

Eagles soar, ducks quack, loons are laughing. Wind blows, rain patters, then there's sun. There are no jets, no trucks in the distance, not even dogs barking—only the howl of the wolf. I could carry on about the clear drinking water, the fog rolling in at evening, and the fragrance of thousands of wildflowers on the wind.

This is a place where I can seek inspiration.

June 30

I'm sitting at a small, wispy campfire with night closing in around me. There is a rustling at my elbow, caused by a little white-footed mouse that's making its rounds, discovering morsels around the campfire that were spilled during the preparation of dinner.

Campfires are mesmerizing. I'm not referring to those early morning blazes that get the coffee and the blood going. Campfires are those crackling tongues of flame that begin to murmur as darkness creeps out of the trees. Their wispy curls

TRUE NORTH

of smoke hang in the air, as if reluctant to leave the pale flames, the orange, glowing coals, and the occasional popping of pine resin.

A loon calls. My thoughts drift to other places, other fires . . . other mice. If there's a campfire, it means that I'm in a quiet place, taking the time to gather wood and sit around watching the fire, either alone or with like-minded friends.

Many stars shine overhead. Cool air presses all around the fire's perimeter, and a moth cruises dangerously close to the tips of the flames.

I haven't seen the mouse for a while. Perhaps it's resting, now that it has a full stomach. I'll do the same. It's time to douse the fire.

A bald eagle literally screamed past as I was standing on a high cliff ledge.

JULY   Good-bye, All You Loons

July 1

It's always difficult saying good-bye to a place you love. Today I drag my feet packing up the last camp, folding the tent just so, and looking across the land to the clouds on the horizon, realizing that I'll travel out there—over that distance—today and tomorrow.

I listen to the breeze and the calling crows closely, trying to soak in the flavor of the place so I can take it along with me. I watch an ant walking with its load and a spider spinning a strand of silk. I'm stalling, really.

I sit on some rocks, and my friend Steve stands on the lakeshore. We're both silent, looking out at the lake, waiting for the silence to be broken. Finally one of us says, "I guess it's time to go." We stand, our minds already set to the future, but I'm still sad to leave this peace and beauty for an uncertain place on the horizon.

My back to the wind, I take a deep breath and sigh. Good-bye, fair weather. Good-bye, little mouse. Good-bye, all you loons.

The rushing waters
of Silver Falls,
Quetico Provincial Park.

July 3

Mosquitoes are arriving. An entourage of 200 to 300 mosquitoes accompanies me when I dare stray outdoors. I see their small shadows against the tent cloth.

The relief my tent affords is my salvation. There are a few mosquitoes in the tent with me, but they're easy targets on the yellow walls. Once I've squashed them, I lay back, arms behind my head; I can finally let down

Turn this picture upside-down
to view the meadowscape
mirrored in the dewdrop.

my guard. I listen to them whine against the outside tent door, appreciating the view out the screen and reveling in the fact that all those mosquitoes are wasting their energy.

I wonder: For how long after a man died would mosquitoes continue to feed on the body?

July 4

I've returned to the cabin, to regroup before the next trip. I've spotted baby grouse and black bears on the hill behind the cabin. Day lilies have bloomed, and there is the musty odor of woods growth. I counted 14 flower species on the pathway to my mailbox— roses, columbines, daisies, avens, bunchberries, thistles, fireweed, and more.

Blink, blink. Blink, blink, blink. At dusk the whole meadow twinkles with hundreds of lightning bugs, and as the light diminishes, white-throated sparrows so clearly sing this day to rest.

July 5

Three young killdeer have hatched, and a fourth is cracking its eggshell. The first baby can run like greased lightning; the second stumbles; and the newly hatched third only falls to the edge of the nest, building its strength during its first few minutes of life.

July 6

The weather has been great for flowers. This morning, dew and rain droplets decorate each leaf and petal, making for some pretty photographs. Waist-high grasses drench my jeans. A chickadee lands on my shoulder, only to discover that I'm

not a tree; it quickly flits away, calling "chick-a-dee-dee-dee."

The day never becomes totally dark. The sun sets below one end of the mountain range, only to rise just to the right of the spot where it disappeared.

Good times are here now. I enjoy a bird's song, a passing meeting with a bug in the grass, a sunset, a rainbow, the smelling of a rose. I enjoy the passage of time.

Diminutive ram's-head orchid, a rare wildflower.

July 8

As I begin my walk a morning fog engulfs the land; my eyes rest on nothing. The sun is a pale yellow disk, often lost behind the veil.

The wind picks up almost imperceptibly; this morning it blows from the south. It passes quietly atop the clouds, below the leaves, and through the fog. A raven rolls in the air.

Minutes later, the sun is shooting sunbeams over the tops of flowers, and the beams ricochet off the dew drops hung on each flower. Through each sunlit leaf, I see the shadow of the one behind it.

Flowers are everywhere—roses, daisies, everlasting, and a myriad of others that I don't recognize. Many of those blooming at my feet don't even have common names. A month ago, I had to scour the dead grasses to find significant plant growth. Today it appears that a flower wave has inundated the forest. What a fine painting it would make!

The sun has swung overhead. Bored with all the surrounding vastness, I kneel to contemplate and photograph individual flowers. To understand the real beauty of a field of flowers, bend close until you see but one.

July 9

I'm sitting outside my tent, taking in the evening sun, when an opalescent pair of wood ducks flies into a nearby pond; off I go with my camera. Afterward a snowshoe hare drops by, and I shoot a couple more rolls. Now a grouse, then a red squirrel—for each I use more film. How barren this landscape can appear to be; but in the next instant, wildlife are scattered as far as the eye can see.

Flowers are nearing their peak. This evening, inside my tent, I watch the silhouettes of flowers and grasses inch across the tent wall. The outline of an animated bumblebee busily fertilizes the flowers just outside my tent. Every evening

A wild (but not necessarily Irish) rose.

another flower species blooms—tonight it's lupine.

Earlier today I washed my hair in icy water. Of course, a single dunking wasn't enough. I had to immerse my scalp several times to remove the suds. By the time I was done, my head hurt intensely, my eyes rolled to the back of my head, and my breath came in deep gasps. But my hair was clean.

July 12

I watch a yearling moose calf attempt to follow its mother. She drives it away. The calf is now on its own.

For the next few months, until it becomes "woods-wise," the yearling may blunder through the forest in an oblivious manner. It may stumble into the territory of another moose—an older, stronger moose even more vehement than the mother in insisting that the calf find itself another patch of ground.

What lies ahead are good experiences—learning experiences. If all goes well, the young moose will find mates, drive away others of its kind, and live to the ripe old age of 20 years.

But for now, it's just a panicked yearling, rejected by its mother.

July 17

Remain calm.

Think logically.

The pilot is three days overdue, but I'm sure it's because he can't find me in today's foggy soup—and gale winds came through here yesterday.

Every time a bush pilot is late for my pickup, I have sobering speculations. Has a war broken out? Did he forget about me? Is he sick? Is it survival time for me?

July 18

The pilot hadn't forgotten me. I'm back in the warm comfort of my camper, although rain continues. There's lots of rain, and lots of earthworms atop the ground.

Why do birds—especially worm-loving robins—ignore worms after a rain? Is it because rain brings out such vast quantities of worms that each bird has eaten its fill by the time I see it, or do drowning worms taste bad?

A snowshoe hare warms itself on a patch of sunlit moss.

RIGHT: The willow ptarmigan, Alaska's state bird.

July 20

You know how the wind blows the leaves of trees, bending them so you can see their undersides? If that wind blows throughout the day, turning the leaves and bringing a haze to the air, the portent is rain—maybe a thunderstorm, but certainly the soaking, blow-through-screens-onto-the-windowpane kind of rain.

Last night the leaf-turning rain came; a white wall of water stampeded through the trees, and the gush of pounding raindrops drowned out all other noises of the night.

This morning the spruce needles are studded with diamonds, grasses are bent with droplets, and puddles dot the paths. I see varied shades and patterns of green across the meadow, over to the hillsides, and finally into the tree tops. Everything is saturated.

Today I'm glad I'm not sitting alone in a tent somewhere.

July 23

This afternoon, from the cabin porch, I see endless lines of cumulus clouds moving on a southerly breeze. Tree swallows twist, a glint of white wings in the lowering sun. A bald eagle soars on the edges of one of the larger clouds.

I can observe a cast of characters from where I'm sitting, at the meeting of forest and meadow. Grasses rustle; two chipmunks race and tussle over territory or dominance; a red squirrel nibbles a mushroom. I'm overseeing the tussling chipmunks, the hummingbirds visiting flowers, dragonflies hovering in the air.

The deerflies are the worst I've seen in years. Young woodchucks don't know what to make of the flies, and their only escape lies in going underground.

I can't sustain my thoughts. There are far too many things to watch—yellow swallowtails, skippers, wood nymphs, and monarch butterflies drift by. Wildflowers are blowing, the bees are buzzing, and the birds are singing. There is a constant parade of life.

July 24

Moose calves are growing rapidly, and are gradually being weaned to an adult diet of summer grasses and shrub foliage. I've even watched a moose relishing a newly sprouted patch of mushrooms.

Dense concentrations of flies and mosquitoes are driving the moose to seek relief in rivers and ponds. Flies can travel faster than moose; in

Chipmunks sound a ventriloquial "clucking" when alarmed.

fact, a moose may lose three ounces of blood to flies in a day. Its ample body provides a generous landing strip, and its ears twitch constantly from the bombardment.

Moose also migrate to ponds to find one of their favorite foods—the water lily. They have been known to dive 18 feet in order to feed on submerged roots, and they can stay underwater for almost two minutes.

July 26

Returning to "the woods" (i.e., with a canoe and tent) after a stint dealing with the usual and sometimes stressful aspects of life is definitely a homecoming. Distant thoughts from yesterday's pressing urban decisions still creep into my mind, but I hope and expect that these thoughts will disappear in the weeks ahead.

Some people liken this going to the middle of nowhere to summer camping as a child. I haul water for cooking and bathing, and I do my toothbrushing from a cupful of water. This morning I split some dead pine stumps, for use on days when the sun may not be shining and the wind

I stood on a high hilltop as I took this shot. The photograph captures a bull moose, the largest land mammal in North America, as it passes through a forest clearing.

won't be warm and soft.

This homecoming is about focusing on wind and weather, preparing morning tea and breakfast, and hearing the forest and water voices that are often suppressed by the crush of daily adult responsibilities.

July 27

There are wood crickets at night. In warm weather, one can approximate the Fahrenheit temperature by counting the number of cricket chirps in 15 seconds, then adding 37 to arrive at the temperature.

A couple of cautions: A cricket doesn't sing unless it's between 55 and 100 degrees, and humidity can affect its song.

July 29

Tonight I sit atop a knoll, facing a creek. I watch and listen as zephyrs—west winds—move in front of me along the creek. The gusts come in from my right. First I hear the poplar leaves rustling and observe their shaking. Then I see breezes crossing the creek, causing the water to ripple and gurgle. Finally, the winds exit through the spruces, bending the boughs and whistling through the needles.

I can hear the wind even after it has stopped—buffeting, pushing, shoving. I remember that I'm very small and all alone.

I've witnessed black-billed magpies like this one nip bald eagle and coyote tails during kills to distract them, apparently in jest or teasing.

RIGHT: A cascading stream on the shoulders of Mt. Edith Cavell, Alberta.

AUGUST The Gift of the Fox

August 3

I've traveled to Pictured Rocks National Lakeshore on Lake Superior, and if not for the sound of waves on the beach, I might believe I'm crossing the hot sands of the Sahara Desert. Sand gets in my eyes, ears, hair, boots, sleeping bag, even my underwear. For every step forward there is a half-step back, as the sand shifts beneath my weight. I sink with each step, making my progress slow and cumbersome.

Just ahead of me on the beach lies a small expanse of water, an obstruction. I try to decide whether I should head into the water and wade through its shallows, or go upland. As I mull over my alternatives, the obstruction vanishes.

It was only an illusion—a trick of the sun. Light rays passing near the hot sand were bent into the cool air, forming a mirage. The actual body of water was a bay still some distance down the beach, but its image was transposed, so it appeared much closer.

I trudge forward in the sand.

A portrait, if you will, of a red fox vixen basking in spring warmth.

August 7

Tell me today of the exciting life of the professional photographer. Tell me of the glamor, the faraway places, and the exotic people I'll encounter. Tell me of the discoveries I'll make simply by going for a walk in this new land.

Today the sun is hidden. It's dark as twilight at 11 a.m.; the air is damp and smoke fumes are pungent. My eyes are red,

Shortly after every extended nap, American avocets stretch their wings.

and with every swallow I taste something acrid. It smells as if the neighbor's house has burned and no one is putting out the smoldering timbers. I've been flown into the central zone of a forest fire.

I would rather be eating in a restaurant and drinking a cold beer. These days of sitting in a tent alone or wandering aimlessly in the smoke are boring and just plain disagreeable.

I've often had a marten overwinter near my cabin, feeding on the meat scraps I discarded.

I sleep late, take naps, and haul water in many short trips instead of one long carry. I piddle—repacking, cleaning cameras, counting film, and drifting off into a world of thought. I'm just biding time.

One day of this is tolerable, but two, three, four is too much! I've caught up on sleep, written all the letters and journal entries I can, and read all the books I brought for a "rainy day."

I know it has been a worthless day when the highlight of the day was washing my hair.

August 10

For the past three days, I've driven from the cool waters of Lake Superior into the tropical humidity and near 100-degree temperatures of a prairie heat wave. As I drove across the treeless grasslands, I noticed blackbirds hiding from the heat, perched on shaded telephone lines.

My shirt stuck to my back and, in turn, stuck to my truck seat. So I found myself leaning forward as I drove, allowing the circulating air to dry my shirt and back. Sunset brought welcome, cooling relief.

This morning I'm watching fog tear apart, revealing a nearby mountain peak, then closing quickly before ripping open again and displaying another piece of the landscape for several moments. The volatile cloud mass is fascinating. I don't really know which landscape forms are poised in front of me, yet to be revealed.

It's as if the landscape is full of magic and sassiness. I'm allowed to see parts of the whole, but I must piece them together. I'm eager to see the mountainscape without its veil.

RIGHT: White pine skeletons, partially obscured by fog.

A lynx, crouched in pensive alertness.

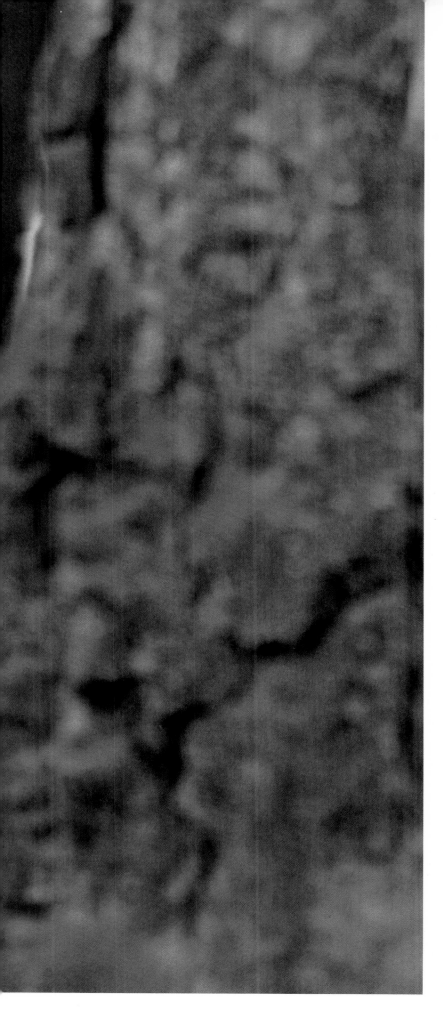

August 11

I'm at snowline on a mountain in Montana. As the snowline melts up the mountain, a line of avalanche lily growth and bloom becomes visible. The lilies received their name for their ability to grow at the edge of avalanche snow piles. In fact, they often poke leaves up through the melting snow.

I walk the edges of snow to avoid crushing any flowers. It would be almost impossible to walk through the blooms without wreaking havoc.

Come autumn, when frosts have turned the avalanche lilies to brown ochre and the nutrients of summer have been stored in their root tubers, grizzlies will scour the slopes, deliberately raking the ground to feed on these roots. It's a mutually beneficial situation—avalanche lilies do well in disturbed ground, and the bears plow the earth at the time of year most appropriate to perpetuate this symbiotic relationship.

August 12

Ah, yes. Tropical Montana. It's 103 degrees today on the north fork of the Flathead River, as I drive through Polebridge.

I hike up and through a large forest-fire burn from three years ago. Fireweed, a post-fire colonizer, has almost finished blooming. Some plants are already seeding. The huckleberries are ripe; I've had them over my breakfast cereal for the past two days.

A little downy woodpecker is prying pieces of burnt bark off still standing trees. No rain has fallen for weeks. The grass is brown, and talc-like rooster tails of dust hang over the road long after vehicles have driven out of view.

August 13

Because the light isn't as pleasing at mid-day, I wait until 5 p.m. to begin my hike into the mountains. Sun-cupped winter snow covers the trail above 7,000 feet. Although the snow is soft on top, I can feel the solidity of the underlying snow drift.

Rivulets course this way and that, watering the wildflowers—heather, anemone, paintbrush, and lilies. Sun reflects off the snow, making walking in a t-shirt comfortable; as I top the shoulder of the mountain, I wipe perspiration off my forehead.

I almost fail to notice a mountain goat billy lounging in a snow pile, chewing his cud with his forefeet sprawled forward, eyeing my progress. Carefully, methodically, I turn my camera toward the goat, clicking the motor drive release when he's in focus.

The sun is warm and the goat has a thick coat, so the snow must feel cool and moist. He can enjoy the comfort as I hike down the pass, looking for other photo subjects and taking in the afternoon light as it falls on the distant points of spruce tops.

August 14

Listen to the woods. Don't take your hearing for granted. When I listen, I hear a woodpecker thumping, bees buzzing, wind in the trees, thunder in the distance, water rushing over rocks in a fast-flowing stream, raven wings whistling overhead, dead leaves knocking about in the wind, and a squirrel clawing up the bark of a tree.

August 15

We're in the midst of an unrelenting high pressure weather system that will not move on. Temperatures are 90 to 100 degrees, although in the north country the temperatures become "sleepable" once the sun sets.

Paper wasps are building an addition to their lamplight nest. The nest will be discovered by gray jays, then chickadees and other small birds after the leaves have fallen and the worker wasps have died. The birds will tear open the nest, eating any remaining larvae and eggs whose development ended with the first hard frost. The work of the many workers will benefit only a few, but it will guarantee the continued existence of the species.

I accidentally uncover a mouse nest that contains five sightless, hairless young. Mother isn't around, and the babies wince at the bright light forcing its way into their dark, damp world.

Animals are scarce. Once in a while, I see a crow or raven panting with its bill open; the deer, elk, and moose wait until dusk to leave their shady hideaways. There's not much to photograph in this kind of weather.

August 16

I wake as the dim light of day brightens the cool, almost cold, interior of my camper. Each morning at about this time, I look outside and gauge the weather. This morning, I see clear skies and sun on a distant mountain.

I have to decide what to do, so I jump under the warmth of my sleeping bag and ponder my alternatives. Basically, there are only two: I can snuggle in and drift back to sleep, or I can get dressed and hike in search of photographs. If I don't get up now, I know I'll feel guilty later— say at nine or ten a.m., when I finally wake to a sunny day and light that's already too harsh and blue for pleasing photographs. So I go for it. I pull on my cold clothing, and up the mountain I trek.

Before long, I shed several layers of clothing. I hike higher and higher, through boulder-strewn glacier tailings, ultimately finding full sunlight in an alpine meadow filled with heather and remnant snow patches.

It's a cliche, but I feel like I'm on top of the world. I'm over a mile high, sitting in the lee of a wind-sculpted, sub-alpine fir. Every path leads down; only two nearby peaks are above my line of sight. I can see so much by simply turning my head: Several areas are receiving rainfall, evidenced by gray clouds that send down blue skirts of moisture; unmelted snow rests on various cirques, while warming valley fog obscures the lowland and all of its trees. To the east is the coming evening, while the sun stands high in the west. This is why I climb mountains.

RIGHT: At dusk, this mountain goat passed me on his way to a sleeping ledge.

August 20

Water rolls off the leaves and patters to the ground in irregular cadence, and the forest is suspended in mists that rise from the earth.

Patches of old man's beard lichen dangle from balsam branches. These knots of mint-green life are fascinating. Each lichen is a colony of inter-dependent cells, some of them fungi and some algae. Without the photosynthetic processes of the algae, the fungi could not feed; without the fungi, the algae would not have a home.

Lichens become food during harsh winters. Deer, moose, and snowshoe hares will eat them—more to fill their stomach than to receive nourishment. I marvel at the simple complexity of the forest.

August 21

Here in the northern forest of southern British Columbia, the Fraser River is silty gray. Its waters push and grind into whitewater, flowing over house-sized boulders. Somewhere upstream, trees growing over an undercut bank must have toppled into the Fraser, branches and all. As the river sweeps the trees along its rocky canyon walls, only rounded posts remain—no branches. The bark is ground away, like the paint from pencils that I sharpened against concrete sidewalks in my younger years.

Rivers are to land what artists are to clay. The constant forces of water shape and remake the banks that try to suppress its expressions. What's picked up at one bend may be deposited at the next, to be retrieved again and again, each particle an element in a perpetually evolving work of art.

August 22

The large fir and cedar of southern B.C. give way to pine and aspen as I travel north into Peace River country. The Alaskan Highway begins here, then curves on through the petroleum and natural gas wells and pipelines of Fort Nelson. The town calls itself "Resourcefully Fort Nelson."

Here the forest of doghair spruce grows. Today, cheery cumulus clouds are everywhere. As the road winds north toward the Yukon, folded mountains with no tree growth up high begin to encroach upon the road, and soon I follow their route through mountain passes and along river courses. Stone sheep near the highway eat minerals from the soil; these sheep are a genetic cross between the Rocky Mountain bighorn to the south and the Dall sheep to the northwest.

Sunset catches me still driving. Light remains atop mountain peaks and in the clouds. Snowshoe hares dot the highway shoulder, feeding in the shadows. As I watch color slip from the clouds, a red squirrel gives one last chatter.

There are hundreds of miles more to the north. Rivers cut through these forests—the Robertson, the Donjek, the Slims, the Takhini, and the Yukon. Huge lakes rest in the woods—Marsh Lake, Teslin, Squanga, and Kluane. Endless miles of pine and spruce grow, joined by twisting willow thickets in low marshy areas. Mosses, lichens, and berries thrive, too, until you reach Alaska and the Yukon Territory. Only then does the tree line find its limit. Dwarf birch takes over, covering the permafrost, and tundra stretches north to the Arctic Ocean.

August 25

By chance I find a small, basket-like nest built in the fork of a balsam branch no more than six feet off the ground. I've passed the same

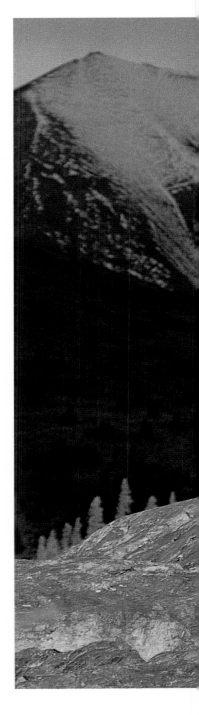

place throughout the summer, and I never spotted the nest before.

I could easily cradle it in the palm of my hand. It's a compact structure of soft bark, plant fibers, rootlets, and hair. Neatly lined with moss stems, conifer needles, and fine grasses, it's decorated with pieces of lichen and bits of hornet nest.

The nest is empty. There are no discarded shells on the ground—they were probably carried away by the parents shortly after the chicks hatched, to prevent predators from finding the nest. I can only guess who the owners might have been, as the frantic activity of feeding has long since ceased—a sign that summer is on its last legs.

Young blackbirds are gathering in huge flocks,

Some people argue that the coyote, also known as the prairie wolf, is more intelligent than a gray wolf because of its ability to expand its range under adverse conditions.

their first staging before the migration south. Other birds, such as bluebirds, will make the trip as a family. Many others will make it all alone.

It seems all too soon for the birds to be calling it quits. Wasn't it just yesterday that I celebrated the first song of the white-throated sparrow?

August 28

For the past several days I've followed a red fox dog, a vixen, and their three kits while they went about their business. As they grew accustomed to my presence, I was able to photograph more and more of their habits and interactions. I was also able to travel with the adults as they hunted. I witnessed several lightning-swift kills of ground squirrels, and even had the good fortune of watching one of the adults act as a decoy to divert a bear away from the den.

After many rolls of film, I was accepted by all five foxes. I sat near them while they slept, followed them as they cached excess food, and traveled with them through grasses and driftwood.

On the day I was scheduled to depart, as if to say, "You're one of the family," the male trotted up to me with a vole in his mouth. He dropped it at my feet. When I didn't respond immediately, he pushed it closer, onto the top of my foot. The vole was meant as a meal for me.

There was much more to this gift than the vole.

August 31

High in the mountains, the weather has socked the mountain peaks with rain for three consecutive days and nights. Creeks and rivers swell to overflowing, and the growling, slogging sound of mudslides echoes from hillsides. Last night the temperature dropped to 34 degrees, and the precipitation changed to wet, heavy snow.

After the past few days of laying low, not being able to search for necessary food, migrating Swainson's thrushes and white-crowned sparrows hop weakly on the ground, too exhausted to fly. Other, not so fortunate, individuals died in the night; I suspect from hypothermia. The little birds can't really avoid the cold dampness and, without food, they can't generate the body heat needed to dry their feathers for warmth.

Nature doesn't plan events; nature *is* the events. The sun and rain, the winds and snows and all the other conditions that prove a hardship for some will benefit others. There's a need to understand the big picture. A disaster for one species can mean the survival of another. In this case, foxes will benefit from the birds' misfortune.

A red fox kit nuzzles its mother, also testing for food odors.

RIGHT: This caribou is a bull, but the female of the species also has antlers.

SEPTEMBER   The Grizzly Encounter

September 1

A female mink is hopscotching, zig-zagging, traveling alternately from shore to drowned tree-root skeletons and back. Her chocolate pelt glistens. A small star of white on her chest complements the white spot on her chin. I can tell she's a female by her diminutive size—males are considerably larger.

I watch from a canoe as the mink swims closer. She explores every nook and cranny, digging for a moment, then carrying what looks like rotten bark or mud to a flat area for chewing. She may be eating small crustaceans that live in the muck. She's settling for small pickings today—mink prefer to eat muskrat, but they will readily eat chipmunks, fish, snakes, frogs, and marsh-dwelling birds.

She eyes the next piece of "land"—my canoe. At the last stump, her mood changes from exploratory hunting to intense curiosity, directed at me and my canoe. The time is right to click my camera.

Click, whirr. Click, whirr. Now all of her attention is directed my way. For many seconds she perches on the elbow of a partially submerged root, before swimming to shore and resuming her sojourn.

September 3

It's afternoon and I'm napping, fast asleep, when a night sound—a sharp twang—startles me wide-eyed awake. What had just tripped or fell

The "up-close" features of a grizzly bear.

Mink pauses on a midstream rock.

against my tent, making an anchor guy line reverberate like a bow string letting loose?

I hear sniffing. Loud sniffing. Deep, heavy sniffing. There's a grizzly outside my tent. What next?

I hear the bear shuffling, but I can't make out its form. I know my 12-gauge is lying next to me in the tent, but I don't dare move, because movement may trigger the bear's "pounce-on-prey" reaction, like a cat jumping on a mouse. So I lay here, hardly breathing, listening.

All at once the side of the tent presses in. I see a circular wet spot the size of a tennis ball—the bear's nose. I see it so clearly that I can watch the tent fabric moving in and out as the grizzly breathes through its nostrils. This could be it; I could die right here.

The tent relaxes. Then I hear the bear moving away. My heart pounds in my ears. Minutes pass. I calm down and grab my 12-gauge. I can't hear the bear.

Carefully, I unzip the tent door. Far in the distance I see a brown rump. I can't help but wonder what was going through that grizzly's mind a few minutes ago.

Coastal grizzlies grow much larger than their interior brethren, due to their access to salmon and lush vegetation.

OVERLEAF: A grizzly forages for food in Alaska's Katmai National Park.

RIGHT: Mountain lions can purr, but cannot roar.

A red maple leaf on moss in New England.

September 7

There are signs of the approaching season. Mice seek the shelter of cabins, the migrators are heading out, and winter wood is cut and stacked with its bark up, to act as a shingle against the weather. Another season passes. Summer feelings are going, going, gone.

Autumn lays her hand over the land. Fruits are ripe. I throw an additional quilt on the bed, and the frosty evening requires that I don a sweater on my walks.

Wasps buzz the air as frequently as flies did during the summer. They're searching for a place to hibernate—not a careless choice, for on that decision rests the continuance of the species.

September 12

A lone sandpiper dips into the mud, leaving small footprints on the pond's edge. Its spotted breast has faded to buffy white winter plumage. It never stops its bobbing motion, a habit that earned this sandpiper a nickname: teeter-tale.

Step-step. Bob-bob-bob. Dip. The routine is repeated all along the mudflat.

Something flushes the sandpiper from the pond. A short burst of wingbeats carries it out of sight. In a few short weeks, it will be skirting the waves along the Gulf of Mexico.

September 19

Moisture-laden air carries the harsh gurgle-caw of a raven passing over the treetops.

The ground is a saturated sponge that squishes in low spots. Near the river's edge, waterlogged pine needles are so soft that a moose could walk on them and pass within 50 feet of me without making a perceptible sound. I like days like this. I can walk through the forest undetected—or at least I feel that I can.

A half-moon brightens the eastern sky by the minute. Immediately after the sun sets, an attention-getting chill sends me for my down vest. Tomorrow morning there will be frost on the fallen leaves.

September 26

It's two a.m. and I can't fall asleep. My mind is restless. The moon is approaching three-quarters full. Maybe the moon's brightness is part of the reason I'm awake.

All through the night, coyotes have sporadically bantered, yipped, and howled. As I write I hear sandhill cranes calling as they pass over the mountains. But the sound I listen most closely for is the stag elk, whistling and bugling. Its calls sound as if they're blown through a bone or glass flute—very primal.

Autumn is my favorite season. There's all this movement—the rut, the migration, the winter preparation. I listen and think, "Oh, what wonder all this other life stirs within me."

There's no smoke coming from these flaming leaves near Lake Superior.

RIGHT: Caribou stands silhouetted against cumulus clouds.

A stag elk whistles during the rut.

September 27

After hearing the elk whistles last night, I want to find a stag elk (not a "bull," as many people say) to photograph and to watch. I often feel that I have to photograph a situation in order to experience it completely.

Parking off the highway, I listen for calling back in the woods. They're vocal this time of year. I follow some bugling to a large stag that's trailing a hind elk (the popular term, "cow," is not correct for a female elk).

I walk along the edge of a pond, coming up behind the elk's flank at a distance of 150 feet. No dice. As soon as I approach the hind elk, her stag directs his attention to me—a hard stare accompanied by a brisk walk in my direction. He is going to deal with me. I back off my course and he changes *his* course, returning to the hind elk.

I attempt to quietly sneak by the grazing elk several more times, with the same result. In rutting season, stag elk (and bull moose) are truculent and dangerous, and they possess the weaponry to move an animal of lesser stature wherever they choose.

Photographs? Who needs them in a situation like this?

OCTOBER Spirits in the Forest

October 2

Walking in the pre-dawn light, I peer into the pines and resplendent autumn maples. It's bright enough to see reds, yellows, and oranges. The sun has barely cleared the hills, and is just visible through a gossamer cloud cover.

Most of the leaves are still attached to their branches. Leaf color is at peak blaze, but the next heavy rain or wind will surely strip great quantities, sending them earthward.

I can't even leave my campground without stopping for photographs at one place, then another. Despite all this color, it's not simple to compose a pleasing photograph. When I find a brilliant tree, there are many reasons that the image I take won't succeed. A major reason is this: By the time I approach a distant tree I'm standing underneath it, looking up at the less colorful undersides of the leaves.

I look for the greens of conifers to place behind a radiant tree; the dark green offsets the bright yellows of sugar maples. Or I search for smaller trees—trees I'm level with or trees I'm above, so I can highlight the upper surfaces of leaves.

The peak colors of a mixed autumn forest in New England.

I spend the entire day doing one thing or another in order to put light on thin pieces of celluloid. I walk slippery river rocks, the rim of a beaver pond, the edges of back roads, and main highways. At some moments, I know I successfully combine the play of light with the juxtaposition of my subjects, their color patterns, and their backgrounds, to capture a

A porcupine wears its full regalia of quills.

photograph. But most of the time I stretch the possibilities of a snapshot, hoping to elevate it to a photograph.

Tonight I'm weary after nine hours of "over the hills and through the woods." It's dark outside my camper, and the roof is alive with the sound of falling raindrops.

I'm quite content on days like this one. I've experienced so many sights, sounds, and smells. The rain at dusk actually gives the day a sense of completion. It's over. It's time to settle, to seek shelter, and to bask in the warmth of memories.

October 6

Just as humans with wood-burning stoves must cut many cords of wood each year, so must the chipmunk hoard stores of cones, mushrooms, and non-perishable seed in order to survive until spring.

I watch a chipmunk searching for food under the leaves, over the leaves, and all between the leaves. It fits one acorn in its mouth pouch and one in its teeth, but there is one acorn left. How should it carry the last acorn? In its forepaws? It's worth a try, but the chippy tumbles, discovering that it can't run with such a load.

Off it goes, only to pause. With considerable trepidation, the chipmunk decides to return for another attempt at carrying the third acorn. After cursory nibbling of the acorn's sharp edges, the chipmunk finally fits the third acorn in its other cheek pouch and scampers away. With its swollen features, it appears to have the mumps.

A few moments later the chipmunk returns to the acorn patch. A weasel, possibly mistaken for another chipmunk or a squirrel, comes within inches of the unwary chipmunk. Chippy is elated by a batch of newly-discovered acorns, and fails to notice the weasel's careful approach. At the last moment, the chipmunk catches movement or scent, and escapes with its life.

The almost unnatural brilliance of wax-gill, or neon mushrooms.

October 9

Already winter's breath coats the northern hill-sides with frost. Puddles glaze with ice. Glacial rivers clear to green and blue from the gray of summer silt.

Gone are the swarming clouds of insects—and the swallows. Gone are the mushy mudflats of summer—and the plovers. Gone are most of the migrating birds.

Darkness comes at 6:30 p.m.; lights from cabin windows poke holes in the shadows of distant hillsides. Sleep comes earlier in the evening and lingers on into the mornings. I'm feeling that summer has departed and autumn will soon pull its cloak out of the sky to let winter in.

October 11

The ground is covered with acorns. Ripe nuts clatter down the branches, often with the help of a squirrel or two.

Gray and red squirrels use different strategies for winter food storage. Gray squirrels are known for their multiple deposits of single nuts. They carry an acorn between their teeth, search for a suitable hiding place, and tuck each nut into the soil with their forepaws. A few scattered leaves over the top eliminate any sign of disturbance.

The gray repeats the process thousands of times each season. If a few nuts are found by another squirrel during the months ahead, the gray squirrel has no problem smelling out others nestled

A "Glacier Erratic Rock" in the Apostle Islands, almost entirely covered by moss.

just below the snow. A gray squirrel can smell a nut covered by a foot of snow, and simply tunnels down to reach the food.

The red squirrel, on the other hand, is a hoarder. It makes large stockpiles of pine cones, nuts, and mushrooms, then must aggressively protect the cache from other squirrels. It has the luxury of eating its fill in a single setting, but if another animal discovers its supplies, the red squirrel may find itself on the edge of winter survival.

October 12

The fox stops suddenly. It rotates its head and perks its ears, cocking its head first one way, then another.

It begins stalking—testing each foothold, putting a forepaw down lightly, careful not to break a twig, occasionally bringing the paw back up and choosing again. To further reduce noise, the fox places its hind paws exactly where the forepaws have been.

With its eyes fixed on a patch of distant grass, the fox freezes, then carefully coils into a deep crouch. It pauses, adjusts its footing, then springs, arching through the air over a tussock.

As it lands gracefully, its forepaws pin a mouse to the ground in the grass it was eyeing a moment before, and mouse becomes fox.

October 14

Leaves alone possess the secret of a beautiful death.

I walk onto a hillside of maples and the ground, not the trees, is gilded with yellow. Bright fallen leaves, still wet with color, stick to my boots. I kick and shuffle, playing in brightness.

Diffused light bounces down through the treetops, reflecting off each remaining leaf until the light completes its journey to the leaves on the forest floor. The effect is one of standing inside a glowing room that's shining from all angles. My only visual relief is the black-stained boles; everything else melts into bright cadmium yellow.

Daylight has slipped to less than eleven hours total. The leaves will soon dry and crumble, returning to the earth, and the nutrients they unleash will set the hillside of future autumns aflame once again. Theirs is a cycle of life, not of death.

October 16

Another sunset. Evening mist rises from the warmer-than-air waters of Wisconsin's Flambeau River, and my breath hangs in the still air. It has been raining most of the day, and I watch the black-tea river roll over and around boulders. Mosses, lichens, and mushrooms are turgid and vibrant. This is their time of year.

Just as deciduous trees rid themselves of unnecessary leaves, white pine and red pine drop spent needles. The brown needles hang like ornaments on the understory shrubbery.

The damp, musky air holds a scent—an essence of decaying leaves. The maple and aspen forest exudes this familiar perfume in the spring and autumn, and I draw in these odors. The northern forest fragrance is one I love. Nowhere else smells quite this pleasant.

October 17

Autumn: A leaf with all its colors eaten to lace.

Leaves drift earthward, stopping momentarily, settling on branches, rolling off in the next gust of wind. Sometimes the wind whirls pockets of fallen leaves airborne again, often to great heights and distances. Does the leaf comprehend its brief moment of glory as a toy of the wind?

October 22

Leaf teepees dot the forest floor. Pulling the small mound of leaves away reveals a hole beneath each one—and in the holes, earthworms.

OVERLEAF: A red fox—the most common fox in Canada and the northern U.S.

Sometimes the teepee maker can be seen slipping back into its darkened chamber.

Worm populations peak at this time of year, as decaying organic material provides plenty of nutrition. In the dark of night, the glistening bodies emerge to feed on leaves. While they digest the decaying matter, they release rich, black castings that serve as the fertilizer of the forest. Up to 18 tons of worm castings are applied to an acre of soil each year. As day begins, the worms round up a few leaves and pull them back toward the burrow. These "teepees" provide both a source of available food and a screen from the invading sun.

As colder weather sets in, the worms will retreat deeper into the soil, burrowing below the frost line. There they'll wait until spring, when the return of warmth prods them to the surface and their teepees reappear.

October 23

I'm traveling north from Hartford, Wisconsin. As I near the Horicon Wildlife Refuge, I see flocks of geese in the sky. Long lines of birds fly in V-formation; in every direction the sky is peppered with skeins at various heights, all homing in on Horicon.

Wherever I hear them, the nasal honks stir my feelings. I often sit on lofty knolls watching geese pass, wishing I could spread my own

Canada geese fill the autumn sky over the Horicon Marsh National Wildlife Refuge.

RIGHT: A whitetail buck pauses beneath a striking display of sugar maple foliage.

imaginary wings and join the flock sailing away from winter's cold.

As sunset approaches, then fades, geese begin to stream into the Horicon Marsh for the night. Flocks pour down in long lines, filling the sky. Geese set their wings on a steep downward glide into the marsh, and some individuals sideslip, turning nearly upside-down in an effort to lose altitude rapidly. Tens of thousands continue to arrive long after the red glow has faded from the western sky. The gabble of avian voices stretches for miles in all directions.

I stop to look into the sky as each flock greets its brethren below. The lines of geese seem endless.

October 24

The silencing of the forest is difficult to ignore. All I hear during my forest walks are a few juncoes, nuthatches, chickadees, and an occasional woodpecker. These are pleasant sounds; it's just that the clamor of growing and living has departed or died. Nothing scurries out of my path as my boots tromp the woods and fields.

This particular silence rings with the songs of voices now absent.

October 26

There are spirits in the Canadian forest—beings that come and go. They've watched me from afar, and they've undoubtedly stepped in my footprints. I can't begin to guess how many times they've stared at me from positions of concealment. It's rare to catch sight of these hunters, and sightings are usually no more than fleeting glances. Today is different, though.

Today I follow a red squirrel darting around the forest floor, searching for a fallen spruce cone. With cone in mouth, the squirrel climbs to a higher perch—a fallen log—where it sits and shucks the spruce cone while casting watchful eyes into the forest.

Suddenly the squirrel begins to chatter. It flips its tail nervously and stomps its rear paws. Something it sees, smells, or feels is making the little squirrel quite agitated.

I look around and spot a cat resting in the fallen leaves, almost hidden in brown grasses. At first glance I think it's a bobcat, but on second look I realize it's a lynx, calmly watching the squirrel—and me.

Realizing it has been seen, the lynx performs a graceful hop-away, trots a distance, then turns for one last glance before disappearing into the underbrush.

October 27

The night blows with the promise of serious cold. Tonight will bring more than a dusting of frost, frozen puddles, and cloudy breath. Thick, gray clouds indicate that snow is on its way.

The time of preparation for winter is about to end. Am I ready for the cold? It's almost too late to ask.

October 30

The river was locked away last night. Thin sheets of transparent ice extended from the shoreline, joining sheets in the middle. The moving water is still visible, but the gurgles have been muffled.

I toss a rock onto the ice, but it only bounces, sending sound ricocheting across the river. I'm tempted to step on the river's edge.

The ice will thicken; its glasslike quality will be replaced by translucency. The sun will not warm the waters for many months, so the creatures that crawl on the bottom or swim in the currents will live in a darkened world. In spring the ice will crack and heave, and the light will return.

LEFT: A multi-colored montage
of fallen maple leaves in a New England forest.

NOVEMBER Between Light and Darkness

November 4

The mountains are capped with snow, and the snowline descends with each cloudy spell. Winter already seems permanent, but as I look at the white summits I know I'm looking at creeks that will rush down the rocks in spring. The vibrancy of spring's green will return in direct proportion to the amount of snow that rests on winter peaks. In the mountains, snow represents new life.

November 5

The pond is steaming in the frozen air this morning. My hands, even in gloves, are as stiff and clumsy as robot hands while I'm photographing. Condensation forms on my mustache and then freezes; I'm not fond of the onset of winter temperatures.

A beaver swims to shore, butting its head through ice half an inch thick to create a series of breathing holes. When the ice becomes too thick for the beaver to break, it will pull aspen branches from the mud below and use them for food. On particularly cold days, steam will rise from the beaver lodge, as the body heat of the lodgers rises through the mud and branches. For now the beaver keeps the ice open, maintaining its access to fresh air for as long as possible.

Hoarfrost, formed when mist from rapidly cooling water freezes onto the nearby landscape, decorates branches and

A mountainscape presides over a frosty river in Banff National Park.

The "simple complexity" of a spider web, this one laden with morning frost.

grasses. Waters are chilling at night, and they can't warm sufficiently in the shorter daylight hours.

Where is the summer's warmth? Seasons have traveled like the crazy, short years. Time . . . that hangman.

November 8

Winter has positioned itself outside my cabin. It waits patiently.

Ice grows in columns from the shores of every lake and river. The bare ground no longer sponges beneath my step, and frost glitters on brown grasses at the start of each day.

On several occasions today, snowflakes fill the air like a burst feather pillow; small clusters of snow are hidden in shade-sheltered pockets of the woods. We're six weeks from the shortest day of the year, but snow will blanket the forest before then.

I watch a fox catch three voles and eat two of them. The third vole is cached next to a lichen-coated rock, for a future snack.

Sooner, rather than later, winter will make a serious move.

November 10

It begins without notice. The air fills with a mist

A red fox demonstrates the proper way to capture a mouse that's hidden beneath winter snowfall.

so fine that it doesn't form droplets. The temperature hovers just below freezing. Ice builds.

Ice armor is everywhere—on pathways, buildings, and trees. The trees creak and crackle in their frosty garments. Branches come crashing to the ground under the added weight. The buds of next year's leaves are cocooned under glass, and seeds that birds depend on are out of reach—visible, but inaccessible.

When the storm is over, the sun breaks through the overcast, transforming the landscape into a blinding sparkle. Suddenly the forest becomes a magnificent ice sculpture.

November 15

I watch the sunset retreat up a mountain. I'm fascinated by the light that climbs up bushes and trees only to vanish into the sky.

The mountain still sees the sun, and I rush to photograph the pink color on snow-capped peaks. The mountain's base has already fallen into shadows. After five or maybe ten minutes, the color is gone except for wispy clouds overhead. As I watch they turn blue-gray, then gray, and soon twilight is all that remains.

I can feel the land pausing between light and darkness.

The pursuit, the pounce, and "mouse becomes fox."

OVERLEAF : The elusive mountain lion, a "spirit of the forest," stalking its prey.

November 19

Winter has begun many times this year, but autumn always fought back. The snow falls and accumulates for several days, then the sun melts it away. November is a seasonal see-saw.

Today it's autumn again. The grasses are a dirty, used brown, not the warm, glowing tan of early autumn. The temperature struggles to reach the mid-thirties.

November 22

This evening I'm walking home from a neighbor's cabin. Not a great feat, since my cabin is less than a mile distant. But tonight is sub-zero, and I'm not dressed for the cold.

Frozen air chills my wrists when I shelter my gloveless hands in my pockets. The cold penetrates my single layer of jeans and nips my unprotected ears. If I had to walk any distance, the cold would penetrate even more deeply.

How fragile I am. This is a cheap reminder that nature takes no mercy on the thoughtless. She has firm rules for survival. I know this, but then again I don't fully learn something until I experience it firsthand. A borrowed plumage never grows.

November 25

Winter's moon hurries the sun to bed. The nights are quite long, but that icy moon makes the hills glitter in the brittle air.

I enjoy standing in its light. Despite my sense of loneliness, there's a subtle sense of serenity to the November night. The light of the moon beckons me to step outside and gaze on its pale face, crisp and clear among the stars.

A blanket of new snow covers hickory trees.

LEFT: A bighorn that truly lives up to its name.

November 29

Winter is the tail end of my year. It always seems that way.

I seldom photograph in the northern winter. It's too inconvenient on most days—too windy, too cold, too snowy, too cloudy, and there's not much light even on the bright days. I have all sorts of excuses. But more importantly, animals are in a survival condition. Their health is usually at low ebb, and I respect animals too much to bother them. If they're busy trying to avoid me, they're not feeding themselves or keeping warm.

"Silent" contains the same letters as "listen," and that's what I do in winter. I listen to the life around me; I listen to my own thoughts and ideas.

Living alone gives me the great pleasure—or the great curse—of having my private thoughts as constant companions. There's no one to ask permission for this or that, and no one to dispute my decisions. I experience kinship in other ways—while standing by the bird feeder at dusk with birds around me, for example. Two Canada jays visit daily for handouts, and a red squirrel feasts on the sunflower seeds I leave on a stump.

Most days, I really don't feel alone.

Crystals of hoarfrost on river ice high in the Rocky Mountains.

The blue jay is related to other jays, but it has two additional corvid relatives—the crow and the raven.

OVERLEAF: First snows of winter atop the rugged Tombstone Mountains, Yukon Territory.

DECEMBER   The Hibernators Have It Right

December 2

It's a long four months ahead. Hibernation is probably the best means of surviving winter, at least from the standpoint of energy conservation. I empathize with small winter birds that have to search and scratch in the snow for seeds. When the winds blow they cling to branches in evergreens, lifting one foot, then the other, to keep warm.

The year-round mammals endure hardships, too. As the snow piles up, travel becomes cumbersome, especially for larger animals like deer and moose. Without their speed, they become vulnerable to the attacks of predators. Not that the wolves, coyotes, lynx, and fox have no problems during winter—their food is often hidden by the snow, and the white landscape offers them little in the way of concealment.

Creatures that migrate must time their departures well or they, too, can get caught in winter's wrath. They may fail to survive their trip if they haven't accumulated plenty of fat reserves beforehand.

The brittle winter sun sets over a stand of arctic spruce.

So the hibernators have it right. Using a thick layer of fat for energy, they bed down and shut down for a long winter's sleep. Their biological clocks set, the hibernators won't stir again until their "alarms" go off and spring is near.

A few pseudo-hibernators like chipmunks and black bears spend most of the winter sleeping, but they stir and move about several times. Their metabolisms don't slow to the

A whitetail buck dusted with snow.

same degree as a true hibernator's; however they, too, live in a suspended state and let winter pass them by.

As I stare at the blowing snows through the window of my "burrow," I feel like a pseudo-hibernator, suspended until winter passes.

December 6

My cabin is in the midst of a multiple-day snowstorm. More than a foot has fallen since last night, and this afternoon the air is so dense with snow that trees several hundred feet distant aren't visible.

While I'm splitting wood, small birds twitter somewhere overhead, invisible in the whiteness. A snowshoe hare hops headlong into a hole covered by soft flakes. I've lost many unsplit chunks of wood to the snow cover, but I'll rediscover them come spring.

December 10

An all-day snow covers the few patches of bare ground that had remained. If the temperature were higher, today would be one of those drizzly days when distant hills are blue with the haze of moisture in the air.

Curiously, the birds left for their night perches earlier than usual, as they will do on colder days. I should have guessed why. The clouds are now gone, and wind is blowing from the north. A three-quarter moon shines down on moving tree branches rattling loose their burdens of snow.

The temperature has fallen 30 degrees since this afternoon; frost forms on the inside of my windows. I zip outside to fetch more firewood logs and take a brief, appreciative look at the moon and stars. Where are the birds sleeping tonight? Are they protected from this wind?

December 13

No snow has been forecast, but slowly the temperatures go from 20 below back to 10 above zero. The mountain begins to disappear under

An arctic fox blends perfectly with the new snowfall.

clouds as fine, delicate sprinkles change to flakes. Fifteen inches of snow later, the combined weight of the flakes causes my roof to groan as the snow compresses.

I often share scraps left over from my meals with the wild creatures. Wilted greens and over-ripe fruit are appreciated by squirrels, hares, and deer. I let meat drippings harden in a pan, then place them in mesh bags for the birds to peck at. Sometimes, like tonight, I even add bones to the animal buffet.

As I'm typing, I hear a clunking sound coming from the front porch, where I left tonight's chicken bones. One of the bones is missing. As I watch from the window, an ermine pops out from the snow to snatch another piece, then disappears for good.

December 16

Tracks on the first snows are a surprise, revealing which critters are living near me. On my snow-shoes, I follow the serpentine indentations of otter trails, the Y-shaped boundings of snowshoe hares, then the straight-line path of a red fox.

Animal tracks tell stories of the forest—who's passing through, where they're going, and what the nature of their trip is. Bird tracks and seeds scattered on the ground near weed stalks show me which plants the birds flop against in their attempt to dislodge seeds. Wing patterns in the

The gray wolf, also known as the timber wolf, peers intently around a young evergreen.

RIGHT: The Columbia Icefield in Jasper National Park, Alberta.

snow disclose how an owl's wings brush the surface before it becomes airborne. Double-crescent moose tracks indicate that many individuals have survived the fall hunting season.

The wanderings of the red fox I've been following give way to a few circled tracks around a brush pile. The abrupt end of footprints, accentuated by a pounce mark several feet beyond, detail the fox's attempt to secure some food—although nothing in the snow tells me whether the hunt was a success.

December 19

Gusts of wind chase snowflakes across the surface of the road, back and forth, seeming to go in no particular direction. In the gusts of up to 60 miles per hour, birds are grounded for the day.

A single raven tries to ride the nor'westers, but it makes little headway. The raven swerves and shoots southward; the winds are in control of its perilous flight.

White-outs are a strong possibility, and getting lost in my own backyard is not an unthinkable idea. Weather conditions dictate staying close to the home fires until this passes.

December 24

Today the winter sun struggles to rise above the trees by 9 a.m., swings across the sky just barely above the mountain, then settles behind the

Willow ptarmigans in their snow-white plumage.

LEFT: A male grosbeak wears a "cap" of fallen snow from higher branches.

cliff by 4:30 p.m.

All through the day, the sun is low enough to shine in my cabin windows, and it moves from room to room. There's a warm glow on the white pine wall boards.

As the snow turns blue in lengthening shadows, the sun vanishes for the day, and I watch the glow in the western sky silhouette the spruce and aspen atop the ridge.

Simple happenings make life enjoyable.

Young lodgepole pines reach toward maturity along the Flathead River, Glacier National Park.

December 26

I'm snowshoeing through open countryside, admiring snow sculptures created by the wind. Every stump is a pedestal showcasing some unique shape.

One of the snow mounds seems to hold greater detail than the others, with small flecks of shadow over its surface. On closer inspection, I'm startled when the snow lifts from the stump and glides across the field on three-foot wings.

This piece of living art, the snowy owl, prefers open country and is rarely seen sitting in a tree. I watch this one fly to the far side of the meadow and land on a distant fence post. The owl turns its head once to peer at me through large, golden eyes, then resumes its clever impersonation of a clump of snow.

December 27

Ice crystals floating high in the atmosphere can create stunning optical effects. Just as raindrops act as prisms to produce rainbows, ice can refract and reflect light into the colors of the spectrum. Imagine a sky full of little mirrors falling through the air.

Sun pillars, sun dogs (bands of light bent 22 degrees to the left and right of the sun), and halos around the sun and moon are all caused by ice crystals. While they're not as clear as rainbows, the various hues are visible.

Tonight at sunset, a red vertical column of light appears to pass through and extend above the sun. This is a sun pillar, and it's most often produced when the sun is low, or even below the horizon.

The countryside had assumed a monotonous whiteness for some time now. Tonight it seems that the sun whimsically decided to add a splash of color.

RIGHT: A mountain goat, perfectly at home on a snowy precipice.

116

JANUARY More to Snow Than Meets the Eye

January 1

The new year brings a fresh carpet of snow. Rugged rocks now look like sleek, lake-polished stones. Snow smooths out uneven edges, creating a tidy landscape.

Pine and spruce boughs sag under the weight of the snow, but evergreens are well-suited for heavy snow. Their branches extend horizontally, or slope downward toward the tips. Lower, older branches are longer and conical-shaped. When the snow adds weight, the branches sag until each one rests on the one beneath it and the lowest branches press against the ground for support.

Close to the trunks, there are small clearings. Here, behind walls of snow and beneath evergreens, animals are safe from the sub-zero cold and the winds.

January 6

I had heard that a person's saliva would freeze before hitting the ground when the temperature reached -50 degrees. The thermometer hovered at -48 today, so I thought it was close enough to conduct a scientific experiment.

My first attempt was from the cabin porch. I spit into the air. The result: a wet spot on the snow. Perhaps a six-foot drop was not sufficient. Thinking I'd increase the distance to give the spittle more time to freeze, I climbed onto the roof.

Arcing my saliva into the air, I heard a distinct pop as the liquid froze before it hit the snow. Now I knew.

On a finger-numbing morning, I took this photograph of a frozen river in Jasper National Park, Alberta.

A sleepy fox serves as a reminder that yawning is a universal activity.

January 10

A cloudy mist swirls into the cabin when I open the door to go outside. The temperature difference between the interior and exterior is more than a hundred degrees, and fog materializes above the floor like a creature zipping in through the door.

January 11

There's more to snow than meets the eye, if you stop to think about it. For instance, snow isn't really white. The individual crystals are transparent and faintly grayish. You can prove this quite easily by looking at a single crystal with a magnifying glass in a shaded location.

In a mass, snow breaks up the sunlight with tiny prisms imbedded in each crystal. The human eye can't distinguish the color spectrum created by these trillions of prisms, so the impression becomes one of whiteness.

Snowfalls differ. Sometimes large, one-inch flakes float gently from the sky. At other times, storms send hard pellets of snow bouncing and rolling across the ground. The Eskimo language contains over two dozen words used to describe different kinds of snow and snow covers.

In 1951, a system of classifying the various types of snowflakes was accepted by meteorologists, using flake shape as the primary means of classification. The crystals are placed in seven basic categories: plate, stellar, column, needles, spatial dendrites, graupel (particles coated again and again with rime) and irregular. There are 32 variations within the seven classes, and countless oddities within these 32. That's why scientists say no two snowflakes are identical.

A single snowflake lying on an open palm has no detectable

The bumps and crags of a glacier, as seen up-close.

OVERLEAF: This polar bear is moving restlessly across the snows of Hudson Bay.

RIGHT: A whitetail in the midst of a winter storm.

weight, but snow in the aggregate is a different story. A thirty-inch layer of dry, fluffy snow, or a six-inch cover of wet snow, contains about one inch of water. An inch of water over an acre of ground weighs 113 tons.

Today, dust-snow is falling, so light and dry that it almost resists gravity. At each step I take a cloud of flakes puffs up, then lightly settles back into my footprints, like dust on a dry summer road. Gently, almost begrudgingly, this most delicate snow alights on everything. It's so light that it doesn't settle on my face; it merely tumbles off as a tickle.

January 13

Distant booming resonates through the trees. The source is elusive until more thunder rolls loudly and clearly up from the lake.

Ice on a lake is a dynamic substance. It's definitely a solid, but the crystals react to the laws of nature, expanding and contracting with changing temperatures. Sunshine warms the upper layers, cold temperatures dominate the middle layers, and new ice is forming on the bottom, so the ice is under varying pressures. The sudden shifts and heaves that result produce "lake thunder."

As I listen to the lake, I begin to notice distant drumming from other sources. Bodies of water beyond the trees are creating their own thunder.

January 14

Snow devils—columns of fine snow blown upward tornado fashion by spiraling winds— abound today. With winds of 35 to 50 miles per hour, the countryside appears to be in the midst of an enraged upheaval. Cabins look as though white ghosts are flaring from their rooftops, so quick are the snow devils to develop, explode, and subside.

A whitetail buck struggles to run in deep snow.

"Snow bombs" of wind come alive in an open field, twisting angrily, moving one way and then often swinging in the reverse direction. They blow into my face, then away, then back again as I stand braced against their assault. Great blowing masses of snow race from the ditches, capturing and engulfing me. At times I have to close my eyes, as snow is thrown in my face and poured down my collar.

Later, the winds die. Clouds move in, and the evening sky releases inches of fluffy snow. Where are the snow devils tonight?

January 17

I follow the tracks of a cow moose and her calf. Aspen, maple, and willow branches are ragged where the two have been feeding on twigs. Several times I find a spot where the calf must have rested.

The cow is undoubtedly "sidling" the calf, teaching it to keep moving in the cold and snow. Without its mother, the young moose would remain in the same area, bedding down for much of the day and eventually dying due to lack of movement and food. Such a death would be the moose equivalent of hypothermia.

This is the first and only winter that the calf will stay with its mother. She's teaching her young one well—despite all my miles of snowshoeing and tracking, I never catch a glimpse of them.

January 18

Mine is the first vehicle to pass through six inches of powdery snow on my way home from town tonight. Big, fluffy clumps of eiderdown flakes dance in my headlights, making driving difficult. It's hard to locate the edge of the road.

Snow is drifting softly near the cabin, settling into sculptured caps atop stumps and boulders. The birds will need help with feeding tomorrow. A porcupine has trailed through the snow to a tamarack in my yard; now there's a growing pile of twigs sitting at the tree's base.

January 20

The day begins with clear skies and a great ball of sun chasing the winter blues from the cabin. Already, the sun rises a full hour earlier than it did a month ago. The birds, too, are up early, waiting for me to fill the feeders. The sun feels good on my back.

From the edge of my yard comes a sound I can't quite place, yet it seems faintly familiar. I look at the cabin and catch a glimpse of light—something shiny. Droplets of water are sliding down the roof. A January thaw!

By nightfall the dripping has stopped. The cold air once again sucks my breath away. I break off an icicle and bring it inside, placing the tapered end in my mouth and letting it melt. I go to bed believing that spring will come again. I know because I tasted it.

January 23

A pair of tracks meanders past the cabin. A line of dainty, cat-like prints, no more than two inches long, come down the path, past the woodpile, and across the pond. As I follow the trail, I catch a whiff of skunk-like musk—the indication of a fox scentpost—and I find a few dribbles of yellow on the snow near a log. It's a signal, declaring that this territory is now in the sole possession of a fox dog and his vixen.

I backtrack the wandering duo and find another calling card placed on a rock in the middle of the path. The scat contains a large amount of dark gray hair, the same color as the voles that frequent the field. Again, the deposit is meant as a "no trespassing" sign.

The dog and his vixen should be courting now. At night they'll lie next to each other on the snow, their tails wrapped around their faces to

LEFT: Evergreens coated with hoarfrost in the Rocky Mountains.

shield them from the cold. If I'm lucky, I'll find their maternity den in spring.

January 27

I follow a fresh set of snowshoe hare tracks to a fallen log; I assume the hare is safe inside the log. As I circle it, checking for tracks leading away, I spot the hare under the log.

It looks peculiar. It appears to be tilted over, listing to one side. Its eyes are open, but it seems mesmerized. I creep closer, and still there's no reaction. Perhaps the hare is dozing with its eyes open? Finally I reach out to touch the hare. It's frozen stiff.

At first it looks perfectly healthy. On closer inspection, though, I find that the fur on its left rear side and leg is scraped to bare, raw skin. Perhaps the hare fell, or escaped a near-fatal encounter with a predator, only to die because the cold penetrated an unprotected part of its body.

I'm reminded that an odd mishap can spell the difference between life and death.

January 29

As I step outdoors to get another armload of wood, I'm greeted by an eerie howl. I feel charged with excitement. Somewhere in the darkness, a wolf is announcing its presence. It may be issuing a territorial call or locating its pack mates—whatever the message, the howl makes me stop and listen.

The wolf is a symbol of freedom and wide open spaces. Many things draw me to it: its tenacity in surviving against all odds; its unique form of pack government; its skill as a hunter.

Another howl echoes into the winter night. I'm stirred once again.

The mink benefits from its own fur coat in winter.

RIGHT: A timber wolf knows the forest's residents by their scents.

FEBRUARY The Chickadee Forecasts

February 3

Tonight is marked by one of those brittle, crystalline sunsets. Deep blue shadows behind snowdrifts lengthen, and the highlighted snow changes to pale orange in the final rays of sunlight.

There's a bitter night ahead. Just stepping outdoors causes my nose hairs to freeze as I breathe. It's so cold that my unprotected ears, cheeks, and forehead ache as the air presses on them. I think of that hapless snowshoe hare I found under the log.

Chickadees are the forecasters of frigid nights. On most evenings they feed until after the sun sets, working the last sunflower seed open before flitting off to their sleeping perches. But on impending below-zero nights like this one, the chickadees feed frequently on the calorie-rich lard I put out for them; before sunset, they have departed into the forest. I'm certain they're seeking more protection than an ordinary sleeping perch, because on bitterly cold mornings I've watched the little birds pop out of old woodpecker nest holes.

A thick coating of hoarfrost on spruces characterizes the Great Lakes winter.

On rare occasions, I've held a chickadee that was stunned after a miscalculated flight into a windowpane. I've wondered how a tiny, almost weightless bird could survive a -40 degree night just by puffing up a few body feathers. Somehow they have enough inner warmth to sustain life.

February 9

The staccato cadence of a hairy woodpecker reverberates through the forest. An old

A chickadee is a small bundle of life in the winter forest.

130

aspen snag offers the drummer good resonance, and another roll rings out. Many birds voice their territorial claims; woodpeckers drum for the same reason.

By listening for the drumming, I make my way to the tree. The woodpecker shies away, hopping around to the other side of the branch. It peers around to size up the threat, then resumes its drum-roll.

February 13

February brings the Snow Moon, named after

the blizzards that often strike during this month. In the region around the Great Lakes, another phenomenon occurs, known as the "lake effect." Large bodies of water retain the heat of summer throughout the winter months, so the Great Lakes are always warmer than the surrounding land. When the moisture-laden air over the lakes mixes with the colder air over the land, precipitation forms—which in winter usually means snow.

It isn't unusual for some areas to receive two feet or more of snow during a single storm. Parts of Michigan's Upper Peninsula are buried beneath an average annual snowfall of 150 inches. That much snow is hard to ignore.

February 17

At moonrise I watch the skeletons of trees throw their ghostly shadows across the choppy, drifted snow. The moon almost blinds me when I look directly at it.

A mouse materializes in my view and bounces punctuating footprints across the ground surface before it dives beneath the sheltering snow.

On nights like these, the winter constellation Orion burns the brightest. I scan the heavens, picking out familiar clusters of stars: Taurus, with its V-shaped head just to the right of Orion; Canis Major, the big dog that follows Orion on his hunts; Gemini, Leo, and the great square of Pegasus. And always the Big Dipper, which is standing on its handle at this early evening hour. Five cup-lengths

Polar bear tracks in the snow.

RIGHT: Sometimes tracks lead to a "polar embrace."

A timber wolf, ever watchful, laps at open water.

from the Big Dipper's pointer stars burns the North Star, Polaris.

Appropriately, I end my inventory of the heavens facing north. North is my home and my way of life.

February 21

The heat from the stove brings more than comfort to a cabin that has been unattended for a few days; it brings bugs as well.

Bunch flies that somehow managed to crawl into the cracks of the wooden walls have been stirred by the warmth. They persistently buzz and bounce in the sunny windows, and their population quickly increases. One fly becomes three, three flies become twelve, and so on.

Spiders creep down the walls and hang from the ceiling. They, too, seem to have appeared out of nowhere. They're more than welcome to any flies they catch.

February 23

A chickadee chirrups on a -15 degree day. Stirred into song by the increasing hours of sunlight, the chickadee repeats its cheery, two-toned whistle over and over.

Chickadees are the most common avian visitors to my feeders. In fact, it's impossible to count how many there are at any one time. As soon as one bird pilfers a sunflower seed, it races off to a nearby perch to break the hull open. In the meantime, several more chickadees have come and gone. The discarded hulls of sunflower seeds litter the ground all around my cabin.

February 26

I use the distant mountain as a weather indicator. It's particularly reliable for predicting snow. If clouds conceal its top, I know the sky is low and dense, and I know the snow will continue.

This morning the mountain is hidden behind a gray veil of snow that sifts effortlessly downwind. There's snow and more snow—the plug has been pulled. Accumulation is waist-deep, and snowshoes are required to navigate anywhere off of the packed trails around the cabin. All the low brush has vanished under snow. When I wear snowshoes, I can touch tree branches that I know are well beyond my reach during the summer months.

For me, snowshoeing is the most practical mode of transportation. It allows access to areas I can't reach in my vehicle; my arms and hands are free to work the camera; and I don't have to worry about going too fast down slopes or climbing steep hills, as I do when I'm on skis.

Today, though, I was in a hurry. I made a foolhardy attempt to walk across the snow without snowshoes, and I was left floundering, trying gingerly to lift myself back up to the surface with one leg while the other was deeply buried. Needless to say, my boots filled with snow.

Weasels, wolverines, marten, skunk, and mink are all related to this fisher.

RIGHT: Spring ice-breakup begins on Lake Superior's North Shore.

MARCH The Standoff

March 4

The snow is dirty. At first glance the "dirt" looks like soot, but closer inspection reveals jumping specks of animated pepper—snow fleas.

Snow fleas belong to a group of insects called springtails, named for their jumping ability. They have a special organ, or furcula, which is folded forward and held there by a catch, much like the spring on a mousetrap. When the mechanism is released, the furcula snaps back and the springtail is propelled into the air.

Now water is melting into the snow, forcing the snow fleas to seek higher ground to avoid drowning. They abound on the forest floor all year long, but only in early spring do we see them so sharply etched against the white snow. Today there are literally millions of them, hopping over and through the upper layer of snow.

March 7

A red squirrel lets loose an agitated burst of chatter. Its tail twitching and feet stomping, the rusty cone-husker is unhappy with an equally aggressive blue jay that's squawking its reply.

The blue jay approaches a feeder full of sunflower seeds; the red squirrel drives it away. The blue jay dives at the red squirrel; the squirrel jumps out of reach. The standoff prevents both animals from eating.

Blue jays are second in command of the feeding rights at my bird feeders, after the bossy red squirrels.

A red squirrel chatters on a stump.

March 9

As fate (i.e., luck) might have it, today is sunny. But fog hangs in patches over the ice pack because moisture is being released from the warmer-than-air open leads—fractures in the ice that expose open water. We're circling in a helicopter outside of Charlottetown in Canada, looking for a safe ice floe to land on that's also near a number of adult harp seals with young. I take aerial photographs as we approach to land on the ice, but the situation requires constant reassessment of light, angles, and the skittishness of the subject. Testing the ice is necessary, too, as we try to land on pressure ridges near the baby seals.

There are open leads all around, and attending mother seals bob curiously in each one. Gradually, the females lose their caution and begin hauling themselves out of the water and onto the ice. This triggers a baying of nearby baby seals, calling to let their mothers know where they are. A female approaching an unfamiliar young will nip the little white stranger; she only wants her own baby.

I find it difficult to maneuver into good positions with the alert young seals. Either they immediately lose interest, putting their heads down and closing their eyes, or they slide off over mounds of snow, leaving me with a "rear-end wildlife shot."

March 10

We helicopter back to the ice pack on another warm, sunny day. My heart is rewarded by the spectacular ice patterns I see from the air, and by the prospect of finding wildlife miles from anywhere.

Today the seals seem to respond to the weather. They're calmer, and I'm able to photograph many seal mothers basking, nursing, and tending their babies.

A baby harp seal lies prone on the ice in the Gulf of St. Lawrence, Canada.

Once I'm out on the ice, the distant world of electricity and motel rooms disappears. Another world—one of blowing wind and crying seals—takes over. The white forms, with little to distinguish them from the snow other than those deep, black eyes and their black noses, also seem other-worldly. They're plump and fluffy, and their turgid bodies are round enough to roll like a soft sausage.

Some of the babies roll and twist as if playing; others sleep patiently. Still others move about, searching and sometimes crying for mother to return.

I see no signs of death on the ice—only intense life. But if a mother doesn't return, no other seal will tend to another's young. It's all one mother can do to nurse one baby. For a 12-day period, females do not eat, but their young triple in weight to about 80 pounds.

March 17

Back at the cabin, I'm greeted by a heavy, overcast day with rain sprinkling, soaking, and settling the snow. The sound of water gurgling, bubbling, trickling, and percolating fills the air. Bare patches of ground are colored in dark hues, ranging from tan to black.

Two ravens are bringing branches to the upper limbs of a broken-topped red pine. Their normal loud, raucous behavior has disappeared, because the ravens build their nest in secrecy. From now until their young have fledged, the parent ravens will fly in silence to and from the nest. In order to misdirect enemies, they'll even land in other trees, then slowly sneak back to the nest under the concealment of leaves.

A pair of whitetail deer, snow-flecked in mid-winter.

LEFT: The raven has a commanding view
of its mountain domain from the top of a conifer.

OVERLEAF: A polar bear crosses
a frozen field near Hudson Bay, Canada.

March 20

Last night the forest was hit by 14 deadly inches of snow, compounded by driving winds. The unexpected white blanket will be tarnished by the starving bodies of newly arrived migratory birds before a thaw can clear the earth again. But some—perhaps most—will survive the cold with a meager supply of food, even if the food comes from my feeders.

Today I'm feeding 300 to 500 birds! Among them are siskins, purple finches, redpolls, grosbeaks, jays, sparrows, and several robins. Corn, bird seed, sunflower seed, bread, and vegetable peelings are gobbled down by these transients. At times I count 200 birds feeding in a six-foot circle of ground. Limbs of trees are ornamented with birds that await their turn to feed.

And the song—I've never heard the air filled with such thunderous chordings. It's sheer joy to watch, to listen, and to know that I'm hosting a small happening of feathered friends.

March 25

After dark, almost like an apparition, the sky flickers. It can't be. But it is—lightning, followed by rumbling thunder. The first thunderstorm of the season offers the familiar sounds of pattering rain. I turn out the lights and sit in the window to watch. Great slashes of white rip across the sky, making me wonder if anything was struck.

When it hits a tree, lightning sets the sap boiling; it happens so quickly that the

A gray wolf accelerates through the snow.

RIGHT: At the last moment before they left, the farthest bighorn ram turned back to look at me.

146

trunk explodes. The bolts can also gouge craters in the earth and split boulders in half.

After every bolt, I begin to count the seconds between the flash and the thunder. By dividing the number of seconds by five, I can estimate how many miles off the storm is. In a few minutes, I can barely count to two.

March 27

After three inches of new snow, we get pinching cold with a glorious display of northern lights. Columns of green light materialize, racing up and over my vision, illuminating the sky, only to quickly transform and reshape themselves. The lights start just above the trees and meet at the center of the sky.

Science offers a fairly uncomplicated explanation for the aurora borealis, or northern lights.

Oxygen, hydrogen, and nitrogen in the upper atmosphere emit light after they're excited by collisions with charged particles from the sun. The colors of the auroral display are determined by the nature of the atoms or molecules hit by incoming electrons, and by the magnitude of the collisions. Molecules of oxygen glow red or green; hydrogen molecules produce a red glow; nitrogen molecules emit pink. Individual hydrogen atoms will radiate green light, while nitrogen atoms glow purple.

The displays tend to reach their peak around midnight. They may create great electric currents in the earth's atmosphere, causing lights to flicker and circuit breakers to trip.

Traditionally, northern peoples have believed that the northern lights were rays of sunlight reflected off the polar ice cap. And a Wabanaki

The arctic fox is perpetually on the move through the winter, searching for mice, voles, lemmings, carrion, or previously cached food supplies.

LEFT: A baby harp seal, just learning to swim, tests its stamina in slushy water.

legend tells us the lights are created when a tribe of Indians living beyond the Milky Way plays a game of ball, using rainbow belts that are tied around the players' waists.

March 28

Spring is putting on a Jekyll-and-Hyde performance. Yesterday morning it was spitting snow, and I was greeted by frozen puddles. Today soft, warm breezes move the evergreens. Rain waters a brown landscape; there are no leafed plants to soak up the moisture.

If previous years are any measure, I can expect this kind of unpredictable weather for a few more weeks. In the northwoods, March usually means the end of winter, but only after a protracted fight; March means the birth of spring, but only after a number of false alarms.

March 30

A bald eagle soars on the winds. The mature bird with its gleaming white head must be returning to its lofty nest site somewhere to the north. Nest sites are used year after year, and attain great size due to the annual addition of branches and large sticks. I've seen a number of eagle aeries scattered around the lakes I've explored in this area.

The eagles time their return to match the breakup of the ice. They'll feed on animals that have succumbed to winter's hardships, but the bulk of their diet is fish. Watching an eagle streak to the water's surface and nimbly snatch a fish without getting more than its talons wet is an amazing sight.

Soon the ice will be off the pond, and the waters will be free to mix with the air again.

It takes four to five years for the bald eagle to acquire its pure white head and tail.

APRIL Final Visions

April 3

In my mind I'm hurrying the first blade of new grass, urging it to break through last year's brown mat. I'm hurrying the small meltwater rivulets, encouraging them to cut through the ice and release the captive pond and river waters. I'm even hurrying the three inches of new snow, asking it to melt at least down to the level I hurried yesterday.

April 4

I will patiently watch all the snow melt—every last bit of it. I'll bide my time, waiting and hoping for a week of 50-degree temperatures.

Geese are returning, and blackbirds and robins. When I visit the woods, I find flowers starting their growth and a pond that's melting quickly. Ground frost is being replaced by muddy earth beneath greening grasses.

I guess I'm breaking down. I long to hear chorus frogs peeping and birds singing all day long. Come, spring; happen fast. I need to see new life.

April 6

I've come a full year, and the day does not disappoint me. Although more setbacks may

A red Canadian sunset.

Lynx are another of the seldom-seen, predatory "spirits of the forest."

OVERLEAF: Cheery, fair-weather clouds hover above Cache Bay in Quetico Provincial Park, Ontario.

be in store, the sun's warmth carries the unmistakable promise of spring.

If all the photographs I'll ever take were compiled and judged, it would be a great injustice to call them "my vision." The total would not represent a fraction of my sightings, for how can I step back far enough to include the sunset, the rain, and the resultant rainbow? How can I re-enlist the black wolf, so it poses near the autumn path where I first glimpsed it? How can I slow the moments that progress too rapidly to be recorded, or recapture the "visions" I missed when I was learning to photograph—in fact, learning to see?

The photographic pulse beats faster in some places than in others. In the north country, it beats madly.

Two black (timber) wolves steal away into the forest.

LEFT: Tranquility in Muncho Lake Provincial Park, British Columbia.

OVERLEAF: The northern lights are bright enough to start birds singing at night. The display of lights can be heard as well as seen—they will sometimes create a "rustling" sound that indicates an electrical disturbance.

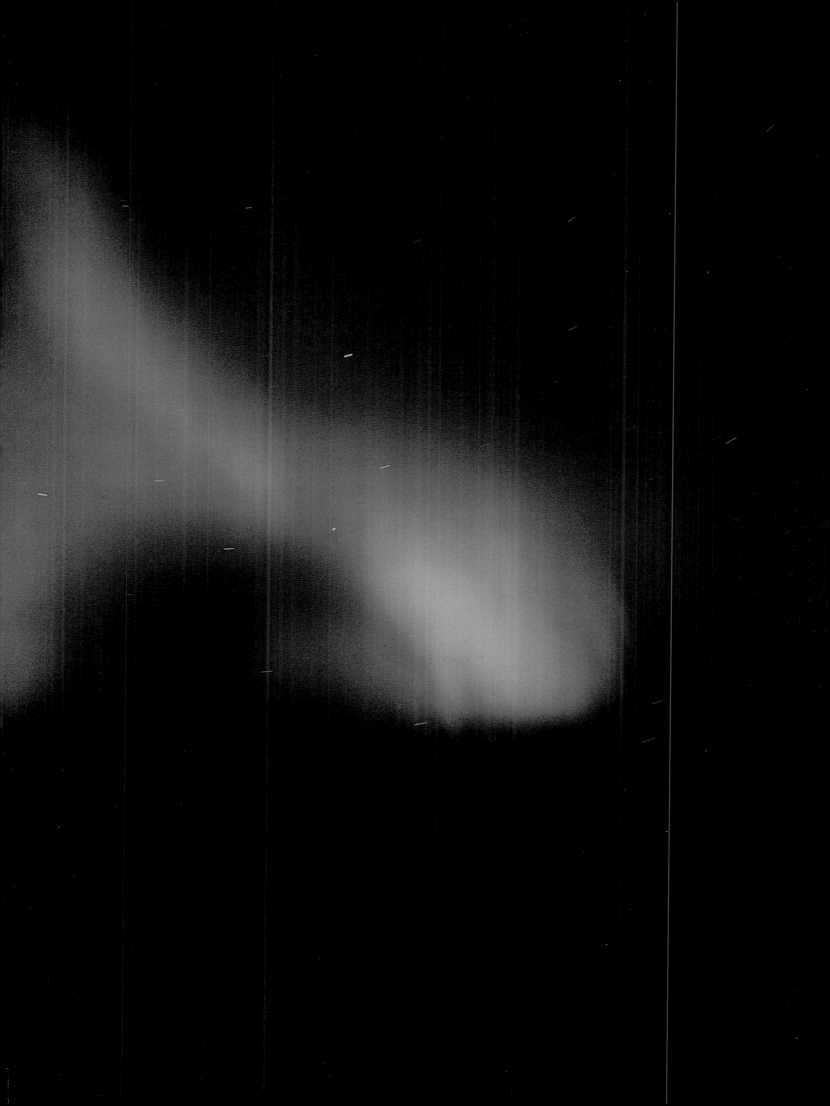